Starhaven
The New World Order of Ale:

C000176412

ALEXANDER THYNN is
divides his time between his stately home in Wiltshire,
a flat in Notting Hill and a holiday home on the cliffs
south of St Tropez. For many years a subject of media
attention because of his individualistic lifestyle, he was
in 1998 the focal personality of the largest ever docu-
mentary series commissioned by the BBC. The 55
episodes of *Lion Country* were so successful that a ten
episode follow-up has recently been filmed.

The cover of this book incorporates a self-portrait of
the author – Lord Weymouth as he was then – in 1990.
The photograph by Bob Caudwell, taken in 1998, is
property of the Longleat Estate Office.

The New World Order
of Alexander Thynn

Views on politics, society and religion

by the Marquess of Bath

STARHAVEN

Starhaven
Box 2573, La Jolla, CA 92038, USA
in UK, ℅ 42 Frognal, London NW3 6AG
Tel: 020 7435 8724
Email: starhaven@aesthesia.co.uk

Designed and set in Kepler by John Mallinson.
Printed and bound by CPI Copyspeed, 38 Ballard's Lane, London N3 2BJ.

Contents

Introduction, by Stoddard Martin

1: Individualism and Society 1
2: Pantheism 4
3: Death, Festival and the Pantheistic Ethic 7
4: Life, and the Assumption of Deity 10
5: Meritocracy Within an Egalitarian Society 13
6: Constraint, and Freedom of Expression 16
7: The Wessex Regionalist Campaign 19
8: Wessex Awake! 22
9: Wessex within a Federal Europe 25
10: European Union 28
11: World Government 31
12: Individualism, Catastrophe and Terrorism 34
13: Warfare and Punishment 37
14: A Charter for World Government 40
15: The Rights of the Individual Man 15
16: Marital Prospects 45
17: The Polymorphous Society 48
18: Pioneering as a Polygynist 51
19: Preaching by Example 54
20: The Purpose of Life 57
21: The Longleat Experience 60
22: Peace of Mind, and Prayer 63
23: Utopia, or Optimism for a New World Order 66
24: Playing God 69
25: Pantheistic Texts 72

Appendix: Speeches in the House of Lords

Introduction

I must declare an interest. Alexander Thynn has been a friend, a chess-mate and a jovial host to me for twenty-five years; thus even if I thought the essays in this volume were not in a style or of a substance I could admire, I might be tempted to publish them. Thynn is a cause. Better known as the Marquess of Bath, he has often been depicted as silly or notorious in the press – sometimes even in conversation by fairweather friends and members of family. These depictions are themselves often silly, unfair and lacking in the generosity of spirit which Thynn has customarily lavished on people in off-beat walks of life or whom he hardly knows. To have in small compass a collection of his views on the great issues of his maturity (he was born in 1932) is to enable a larger public to see him for who he is, to know the warmth of his feelings and to draw its own conclusions as to how silly they are or are not. Many may come to the view that, despite a well-cultivated grand bohemian exterior and partiality to an apparently Falstaffian lifestyle, he aspires above all to be a responsible citizen, a democrat and a philanthropist in the full sense of those terms.

There are inevitably collateral issues raised by a book from an author of this type. In the first place, following a century in which the aristocratic principle has been under near-terminal attack, some may find it appropriate to ask what a man of Thynn's class and background has to contribute of significance overall. Why should we care about the pieties, however sincerely held, of someone so unrepresentative? One is tempted to retort that Thynn may not be so unrepresentative as all that. In any case, he himself has long been sympathetic to the structural scepticism these questions raise. He was opposed to continuance of voting rights for hereditary peers in the House of Lords. Indeed, abolition of those rights in 1999 was the fruition of a policy he had long advocated. In the meantime, when he was a member of that chamber and taking the Liberal Democratic whip, he conducted himself with characteristic aplomb, making contributions to debates which surprised the scoffers with their seriousness, aptness and invention. (The reader may find them here printed as an appendix.)

The truth is that, despite his well-known use in selling scandal-sheets, it is neither fair nor sound to dismiss Thynn as a clown or a fool. He is at least as often that *rara avis* which perhaps is the best justification for his species at large at this stage: a bright-plumaged bird who flies high and on his own trajectory; a free spirit and thinker who tries to discover the world anew and make it over partly to suit his own image – or at least the specifications of his individual needs. He is, in short, an eccentric, perhaps a 'genius' in some olden sense, and partly and always a guileless and occasionally bumbling quester for a holy grail. He seeks because he can. We who can't, or who can't with such scope and ease, might to be grateful for some of his more intrepid forays, if not always in agreement with the insights he brings back from them. Even those who find his views half-baked or perhaps dangerous will, I suspect, not reject them as lacking in 'candour and empathy' – the touchstone values he favours.

What has he sought for, this inveterate quester? Only the answers to the great riddles: how to organize the world best; how to understand the universe; how to find oneself and make one's individual way by paths which impinge on others the least; how, in a word, to *live*, with whom and by what kind of ethics. Much of society – certainly most of Thynn's class – has traditionally taken a view that these riddles have been confronted before and the answers collectively agreed on over time are probably the right ones. But are they? Is it ever safe to stop and rest in the nets of one's ancestors' knitting? This way lies ossification and inertia; smugness and complacency – the least attractive features of the tribe, which Thynn has tried to efface, at least from himself, throughout his adult life.

In taking on the 'big issues', he displays a refreshing lack of petti-ness. 'Anything less than the all-embracing might be a pretention,' a sage once wrote: it might be a useful defense against the charge that Thynn at times exceeds his competence. But then he is an oxymoron: a modern antique: a high-born man-of-the-people. Not only in his friendships but in his words he demonstrates this again and again. By instinct a unifier, he will neither propose nor tolerate an *them* vs *us* point of view. To be 'non-U' in behaviour worries him not at all. To worry about such things would be to adopt a kind of petty bourgeoisness of the spirit. To bring together the high and the low, the duchess and the whore, has been his Balzacian practice. And why not? He is one of nature's kindly spirits: indulgent to a fault of others' eccentricities while censorious only of their needless unkindnesses.

He has, despite rank (or perhaps because of it), suffered much obloquy. Envy creates cruelty: he has known it close at hand. His autobiography – great in the sense of size at least – will attest when completed to the torments, some self-inflicted, others not, which he has had to rise out of since teenage. The heroism of his quest, if one takes it as such, might finally lie in this: a simple doggedness to keep looking at every detail of his life, keep inspecting his motives, keep writing, keep painting and keep forming his particular personality despite ridicule. Publishers over the years have rejected his scripts with a regularity once meted out to the renegade aristo Shelley. Middle-brow art critics have derided the murals with which he has decorated the walls at Longleat. But in the great mass of creation he has erected around himself – these paintings and writings which have filled his industrious decades (and few could claim to have worked longer or with more 'Stakhanovite' discipline, as one friend has called it) – there are perhaps clusters of enduring interest.

One might cite his 'Ages of Man' or 'Ages of History' series of murals; the novel *Pillars of the Establishment* or novella *The Carry-Cot*, the latter somewhat unnecessarily cheapened by its incarnation in film (the idea of Thynn's persona being portrayed as effeminate and foppish shows how blithely he can be misconstrued or misrepresented). One might cite passages of the above-mentioned autobiography, *Strictly Private*, an abridged version of which is on view on his website (Thynn has kept abreast of the electronic revolution and is something of a pioneer in publishing in this form). Finally one arrives at some of the self-confessedly utopian visions present in the political, religious and sociological opinions collected in this book. About them, one or two comments:

Regarding his most high-profile political cause, it has been alleged by another supposed friend that he only adopted regionalist ideas because he fancied himself becoming 'king of Wessex' one day. This is the type of calumny-posing-as-wit to which he has traditionally been subject. In fact, more than a quarter-of-a-century after his regionalist efforts came into in full flower, devolution again became a major constitutional issue in Britain; meanwhile, a Europe of the regions had grown into an irrefragable reality. A world organization of 500 continentally-suborganized regions is yet to come, but most sensible observers are likely to agree that we *do* require states of more equable size and weight, and opposition to this by the hegemonists of the present may become more and more of a target in our new millennium.

Regarding personal morality, fair-minded observers may recognize that Thynn's highly publicized views on marriage, child-rearing and matriarchal social constructs are more in the vanguard than is commonly admitted. Recent decades have produced bevies of would-be moral leaders preaching the sanctity of old-style marriage and family-life while having their eyes, if not hands, on the nearest fanciable bottom. In this respect, Thynn replaces cant with candour. He lives out and speaks out about what he calls polygyny while others play 'slap and tickle' (a pastime once extolled to me with a wink by a female representative of the Crown) and then deny they could ever have had such a thought. 'Hypocrisy is the only weapon the English climate cannot rust,' Byron once wrote. Thynn's forthrightness seems by contrast to be made of non-corrodible steel.

Is he stubborn? Is he naïve? I have said so, at times. And at times he would admit to both himself. But naïveté is a small sin when allied to a child-like sweetness of aspiration; and stubbornness may be a virtue when directed towards a world fairer, more honest and inclusive. No doubt some will see Thynn's visions as belonging to nursery-tale realms; but against the cynicism of received, conservative 'grown-upness', how refreshing they can sometimes be! And how wonderful would be a universe imbued everywhere with a godly divinity such as his pantheism would have it! Isn't this after all what Wordsworth was after in his exaltation of infant consciousness in the great 'Ode' and 'Tintern Abbey'? And isn't Thynn, finally, one of those remarkable children-in-age who have managed to preserve the 'clouds of glory' against time, decay and 'experience' in Blake's terrible sense of that word?

As these allusions suggest, he is in some ways a classical English romantic. His thoughts suggest this in not only their content but also their sometimes archaic expression. Nor have we troubled his garden with too much editorial weeding: too much clipping or gelding or otherwise 'making right' of his words, as Byron complained to his publisher that politic friends sought to do with his more radical pronouncements. The object here is to display Thynn's propaganda on its own terms: his fanfares and clarion-calls from their own happy arena of pomp, yet odd lack of pretence. Falstaff-as-philosopher mixed with Fabian flower-child, he makes his case for a fond and perhaps *au fond* not altogether unrealizable – or, as time passes, unrealized – 'new world order'.

1

Individualism and Society

The general shape of my attitude came together during my years at Oxford (1953-56), but more particularly during the seven years of (occasionally broken) reclusion which immediately followed. I was in a state of disillusionment with all and sundry, but most of all with myself. I had failed to prove that I had any intellectual merit in my final exams, and I had woken up to the fact that the attitudes which I had accepted from childhood were virtually obsolescent. I needed to somersault in all areas of my previous outlook – which is to say on key values: religion, politics and family morality – and to come down into new positions which I might feel confident of holding for the rest of my life.

In some respects I was still concerned to retain my place within the tradition of moral values to which I had been raised – a tradition where there was a premium on kindliness of disposition, in a vein of 'Do as you would be done by'; also on the pursuit of general happiness and a tolerance of the vagaries in other people's behaviour so long as it didn't detract from general social well-being. The particular requirement so far as I was concerned was to discern values which might fortify me in my efforts to emerge as the individual that I believed myself to be, without antagonising myself from the ranks of humanity as a whole.

The essential idea was to learn how to be true to myself. To do this I had to establish defensive bulwarks around my various stances so that I could no longer be brow-beaten by those who had been emotionally close to me during my upbringing. An attitude of individualism was what I needed to develop. In personality I was excessively introspective and self-centred perhaps, so contemplation on these subjects had already been exercised. Still I had to bring the various threads of my thinking together so that its cohesive logic became self-evident.

I had no wish to adopt some brand of individualism which might seek to promote my own interests above those of society. What I desired was to comprehend (and empathise with) the way society had been gradually coming together over the course of history into a vaguely unified core, while managing to perceive the safeguards necessary to encourage the potential fulfilment of each individual personality, and especially my own. It was an attitude which I might now described as a quest for individualism within what I recognised to be a slowly centralising collectivity.

There was a danger that I might perceive this implicit dichotomy as irresolvable and thus feel obliged to take up cudgels against the forces of centralisation so as to promote greater prospects for the liberty of individuals to act as might suit them best. It would of course have been possible to advocate any manner of suspect values under a banner of the interests of the individual as paramount. There was much in my personality to prompt such a course, not least the paranoid tendencies which convinced me at times that society at large (or at least particular members of it) were ganging up against me to disseminate tales indicative of my attributed outsider status. Even at this early date, the tabloids seemed to be orchestrating such a conspiracy. But I managed to perceive that this would not be the wisest solution for me. I had to discover my new set of values from within the notion that man can be at one with larger aggregations of men and that his values should reflect this. It was a question of endeavouring to perceive where the two sets of interest, of Self and Society, might be rendered compatible and even in harmony.

Within this line of thinking, my attention came to focus upon the values of Candour and Empathy[1].

This focus might best be explained in terms of what I was coming to regard as the ideal society. The individual, I believed, should strive to acquire an ability (and the daring) to reveal himself in his entirety for society to have the capacity to understand him comprehensively. The other side of this coin was that those who represented society in its many institutions ought to strive to develop an ability to place themselves in the shoes of each individual who rendered himself transparent for their analysis. Provided that the officials of state could develop this capacity for empathy, then the individual could afford a display of total candour which otherwise he might judge ill-advised.

To present an extreme situation, the worst serial killer in our midst ought to be in a position to know that, if he were to give himself up and explain his anti-social behaviour to the best of his capacity, then the authorities who had him in charge could furnish him with the psychological assistance and supervision required to emerge (for the first time perhaps) as a useful and reintegrated member of society.

No one can expect the full emergence of these values in our day and age and with society such as we find it. But in my own vision, they provide an ideal of society in the direction of which I believe we are gradually evolving. The limitations are implied in the query as to which should come first: the individual's candour or society's capacity for empathy? It is a chicken-and-egg situation which discourages bold improvisation from the one direction or the other. But it leaves me in any case striving to develop an attitude of true candour, in the hopes that society at large will then make its (infinitesimally small) shift towards an enlargement of its capacity for empathy – until (after centuries perhaps) a discernibly new pattern of human behaviour might just conceivably start to emerge.

[1] Subsequent to writing the above, it was brought to my attention that the ideal of Candour might be employed as an excuse for intrusively insensitive comment as a form of aggression, which clashes with any sincere attempt at practising Empathy. For this reason I have modified the original motto, so that it should now read as 'Empathy and Candour – with Tact'.

2

Pantheism

I felt guilty about offering myself for confirmation in the Christian Anglican faith during the time I was at Eton. I had in fact obtained a distinction for Divinity when I matriculated for the (old-fashioned) School Certificate. But my doubts concerning the validity of messianic claims, no matter which religion I might examine, rendered me sceptical concerning the nature of the God(s) whose worship they proclaimed. I also respected my father's atheism, much vaunted at the time – although he was to become a follower of Bagwhan in his later years. Then at Oxford I became acquainted with humanism, which impressed me for its greater reverence for truth (as disclosed by science) and for setting squarely upon man's shoulders the responsibility for sorting out the world's problems. But I retained some doubt as to whether the human race might really have any right to assume that it was the highest form of life within the universe and that it would necessarily remain pre-eminent here on Earth. I feared that we might engineer our nuclear extinction, leaving this planet for the exploitation (or wiser control) by some other species, be it dolphins or cockroaches.

The solution as I perceived it was to evolve my thoughts from humanist doctrine, to reintroduce the concept of deity. This I would do by formulating a means of venerating the universe (which contains all imaginable species) to the point of worshipping it. Within such a faith, it could be the totality of the universe – the Cosmos – which would emerge as our deity or as God, no matter whichever religious doctrine we chose to study. God didn't create the universe, God is the universe – so went my thinking.

The tradition of identifying God in this light, looking back at least as far as Greek philosophers, if not to Syria and Egypt before that, belongs to pantheism. Worship of 'the All' may originally have been closely identified with nature, but during the 18th century the totality of the universe became the object of reverence for European writers. On this matter, I discovered that there was dissent between pantheists and panentheists, with the latter proclaiming there was still a distinction to be drawn between God and the universe which he created. My own line became more strictly pantheistic, disclaiming that there could be any such dichotomy.

My position required for its validity a concept of the universe as finite and existing within circuited dimensions of both space and time, so that it could be perceived as self-sufficient, with no need for postulation of any extraneous deity; no requirement for a Creator, Regulator or Intermediator. The universe itself could be shown to accommodate its own such situations, although not always with pleasing results.

The cosmology I adopted runs as follows. The universe came into existence from the singularity of a monoblock, which comprised all matter within the universe under such compression that even its atomic structure was eliminated. This triggered the Big Bang, with matter (in the eventual form of galaxies) exploding outwards on widening trajectories throughout space. The initial premise for a universe of circuited dimensions is that if a straight line is extended indefinitely, it will eventually reach the point of its departure; from this we might conclude that all the departing galaxies would extend their trajectories until they reached a point of universal gravitational collapse. Travellers within the galaxy at that point would perceive ahead of them an imploding wall, which would in fact be their vision of the monoblock from time past. All matter within the universe would at the point coalesce (for a second time) into the monoblock, which itself would then trigger a second Big Bang and second identical history of the universe, which would inevitably include the identical life histories of all the individual people who populated (or will populate) our existing one.

This pattern I could accept as what the universe might be in all its permanence and perpetual repetition. Since there would be no valid distinction to be drawn between the first, second (or any other) repetition of the universe, we could regard them as the same event, with nothing more than a numerical distinction to be discerned between them. The notion of infinite extension through either space or time could thus be eliminated. Even in mathematical terms, where infinite is defined as $(n+1)$, the notion could be rendered absurd by positing a value for 'n' which represents the totality of the universe: the great All. It thus becomes an oxymoron (or a contradiction in terms) to start talking about 'All plus one'!

Some problems remained for potential discussion, such as the apparent contradiction between concepts of free will and fate within the established bounds of such a universe. But these were issues best investigated under the heading of semantics and resolved according to whether the definition for free will or for fate be given precedence in subsequent discussion.

Broadly speaking, I have now indicated what I understand by the nature of God, in that the universe itself commands a veneration that amounts to worship. What I have described might be regarded as an outline for a religion of the future, or more probably as a monotheistic umbrella faith which, over the course of the coming century, could serve to unite the existing religions of the world into a closer form of union than has been the case hitherto, with the common ground being in our identification of God (Allah, Jehovah or whatever) as the universe itself. In this future era there should emerge a new spirit of tolerance between opposing creeds, with each of them continuing its practice in the same tradition as before but at last with a sense of recognition that we are all involved in the same act of worship. This will mark a gradual coming together of our world's different cultures within the same spirit of communion.

3

Death, Festival and the Pantheistic Ethic

I have described how pantheism might well emerge as the religion of tomorrow, but I shall now be considering the special nature of the pantheistic ethic and how it encompasses the ideas of death and extinction. For example, how might a pantheist treat the concepts of an afterlife, resurrection or reincarnation?

I did play around with these ideas in my second (published) novel, *The King is Dead*. It took the form of a science fictional account of how the population of a planet in some far distant galaxy, way out there, was in the process of watching us here on earth, with the assistance of super-telescopes which had such a degree of accuracy that they could perceive the cell structure in anyone's body, to an extent that they could replicate the nucleus from a cell and literally clone any one of us onto that distant planet. Once they had re-created this identical twin to myself (or yourself) up there, they would be able to feed it with our personal memory of the life we had led here on earth, since they would have it all recorded on tape, so to speak, over the prolonged course of time during which they had been observing us. There would be no way for you or I to distinguish between the person that we once had been down here on earth and the person we found ourselves to have become up there.

I am still not clear whether the ideas that I introduced into this novel should come under the heading of reincarnation or resurrection. Not that it really matters of course. It merely stands in illustration of the fact that I cannot regard such matters as a total impossibility. But I feel more comfortable in regarding the subject of death in a different manner.

I prefer to perceive my life as part and parcel of the permanence which constitutes our universe. I have my niche in it, and my task is to reconcile myself with the existence of this life, standing as it does in perpetuity within that universe. In doing so, I might hope to discover my peace of mind.

With regard to the essential ethic for a pantheist, there are always two poles of thought which need to be brought into consideration. They concern on the one side the individual and on the other the totality of the universe which contains him. On balancing the best interests of a person's individualism against the best interests of society at large (which is to say the universe as a whole), the recommended codes and precepts for moral conduct may gradually be worked out. That is what lies at the heart of the subject.

On the one hand we require extensive reading (or study in the field) of individual psychology. On the other, the necessary reading should be on the sociology of human populations, or the ecology of our planet – coupled with an acquaintance of theories on the nature of the universe. The problem once again is how to obtain the maximum bloom of individualism while keeping it compatible with the best interests of society at large.

As to a purpose in life, a pantheist might reason that it is to discover his own sense of integration with the totality of the universe: to perceive his niche, and to fill it to the best of his ability. The conception of a niche might be an ambitious one or on the most modest of planes. The local woodsman or plumber is entitled to as much self-pride in the performance of his prescribed duties as the landowner who employs him. We all stand in service to society and to the universe which contains us.

Even if pantheism is to emerge (as I anticipate) as an umbrella faith for the existing monotheistic religions of the world, the ethic peculiar to each individual religion may of course remain predominantly intact. Tradition counts more weightily in these matters than any amount of logical innovation. More explicit conversion to pantheistic ideas will depend upon how much scepticism develops concerning the tenets of faith within a particular religion. Whenever people start to doubt in such matters, the focus is liable to shift in a direction where the scientific emphasis might appear more sound.

As the practice of global pantheism emerges, there is likely to be no radical change to the calendar for special days to celebrate within the year. Easter will remain peculiar to the Christian tradition, Ramadan to the Moslem, Passover to the Jew, Janmastmi to the Hindu and

Death, Festival and the Pantheistic Ethic

Dharma Day to the Buddhist. But special days for pantheistic celebration could well emerge, perhaps corresponding to these points on the solar calendar, such as the winter and summer solstices – indicative as they are of natural points in the seasonal cycle of each year, to be observed after careful note has been taken of the way in which our planetary system (if not the universe itself) functions.

Diversity in religious celebration will still flourish as long as we rejoice in our individualistic cultural practices. Under the aegis of pantheism such variance should not only be tolerated but actively encouraged. The community as a whole benefits from the contrasting input of its associate members. And in our discovery of the way in which this spirit of co-operation emerges as a reality, the full richness of a new religious order will gradually become apparent – until the spiritual unity of mankind has genuinely been attained.

4

Life and the Assumption of Deity

Pantheists have much to learn from humanists in their approach towards human life, but the emphasis upon other forms of life (both on this planet and elsewhere) needs to be kept within the focus of our attention as well. I discount as a statistical improbability the supposition that our human species is unique in its intelligence or for the potential role it might play in the history of this universe. But in the absence of any proven contact between ourselves and extra-terrestrial intelligences, we should be prepared to assume all the responsibilities that the evolution of our own intelligence appears to demand.

Along with that intelligence, we have developed the capacity to assist other species for altruistic reasons; but we are only just beginning to discern what manner of actions we should take in order to save from extinction whatever is endangered, or indeed to ensure that the environment on this planet remains salubrious enough to support living creatures. Slowly we are learning to perform what is required of us in this regard. As we do so, whether we like it or not, and at the expense of laying ourselves open to the charge of hubris, we are assuming the mantle of deity.

Something which conflicts outrageously with this identity is man's acceptance of himself as a carnivore. For us to nurture other creatures with a view to fattening them up for slaughter, and then consumption, undermines any possible argument that we have their best interests at heart. We become an unpleasanter (and less admirable) species as a result of our meaty indulgences. Nor shall we truly be in a position to assume this mantle of deity until our feeding habits have been changed.

What might appear today as too sizeable a problem (to adopt a diet that is both sufficiently nourishing and sufficiently exciting to compensate for the absence from it of any meat) will no doubt become a lot easier as we advance through the new century. Once scientific research has come up with the means of producing a substance (edible fungus perhaps) which displays a similar texture, taste and variety to the flesh that we have grown accustomed to eat, then I anticipate that the transition of man in his cultural practice from carnivore to vegetarian will emerge as its natural consequence. In the meantime, of course, like the rest of humanity, I shall in all probability continue to indulge in obscene flesh-eating habits.

Even in our imperfect state of spiritual evolution, humans should not flinch from this role in life of consciously assuming the mantle of deity. At the least, it is one we should assume until such a time when a superior intelligence has been scientifically discerned – at which point it (or they) may lift the responsibility from our shoulders. This position will of course give rise to debate on the extent to which we should exercise our capacity to alter things from what they might otherwise be or have been. A lazy belief that when we alter things it can only be for the better always lies open to protest from those who view too much change sceptically.

The most controversial area arising from our playing at deity has to do with the the sanctity of human life, especially as it relates to issues such as birth control, abortion and euthanasia. Within the pantheistic ethic, there is no such sanctity to be recognised *per se*. It is even conceivable that murder could be justified under most exceptional circumstances. The criteria for determining these cases (no matter which the issue) lie principally on the pragmatic plane – i.e., of discerning where the greatest reduction of human anxiety is involved and the implementation of the greatest general happiness achieved.

Until such a time as generalisations can be effectively established, these questions should be left largely to individual case study. The human anxiety which derives directly from unwanted pregnancies, and from overpopulation, should certainly be factors weighed heavily when it comes to any final assessment of such matters. But the balance becomes distinctly more marginal if (for example), when considering the justification for abortion, nothing other than the family planning of the parents is concerned. Humans must not shrink from the necessity to play God in the making of their decisions. Where a pattern of greater potential happiness (or peace of mind) is perceived as a result of taking such a life, then a pantheist's persuasion should be to proceed.

It will remain important, of course, to discern and retain the criteria for judging if there has been abuse of the license to suppress human life. The guiding rule perhaps should be that we remain careful in all cases to avoid implementing our own moral judgement in contradiction of the established rulings. This is in effect saying that we should respect the law no matter how hard we might be trying to get it changed. To behave otherwise merely opens us to the charge of supposing that we are a law unto ourselves. In recognising the law of the land as a shield against total anarchy, I submit to its regulation of my conduct in this life until the desired change in the law has been brought into effect.

Mankind may have a glorious role to play in the continuing history of this universe, provided that we can see our way to act as the agents for all living creatures, in the realisation of their use and dignity within the evolutionary process, where we all have our allotted space. There is no special privilege within this discovered role, but we may enact it as we find it for whatever duration it may last. We should assume that sometime, somewhere, the role will be taken out of our hands by others more worthy of it. In the meantime we should play it to the utmost perfection of our ability, in the hopes that such credit as will accrue to us will stand, within the permanence of time, as our everlasting memorial.

5

Meritocracy within an Egalitarian Society

Envy in the human heart will not gladly tolerate the superior wealth and privilege that may fall to the lot of another person, especially when that person displays less merit. Such inegalities have perhaps engendered more social unrest than any others over the course of modern history. Theories for redistribution of wealth have, however, been found wanting in practice, inasmuch as they have failed to bring about either a just society or an egalitarian one. Many attempts at these ends have been wildly misdirected. There may be greater scope for improving the nature of society if instead we seek to rationalise who gets what and for which reasons.

Since time immemorial there has been evident social distinction between those who have and those who have not. Nor is this a contrast that can be entirely eradicated, due to the intrinsic nature of man. Talent is not uniform in its distribution any more than are the environmental conditions which prevail over the course of any child's upbringing. Psychological advantage of one kind or another cannot be totally eliminated; but there is still a great deal that can be done to ensure that advantages cannot be bought, so as to enhance the opportunity for all young adults on emerging from their years of education to embark in a spirit of fair competition towards the attainment of life's prizes.

The initial point of concern is that funds from the Inland Revenue should not be used to subsidise any system for private education, apart from those schools which are recognised as necessary for rectifying the imbalance in privilege for some disadvantaged minority. I have here in mind the concept of special schools for recent immigrants or for the disabled. As a general rule, however, if a minority group (whether social, ethnic or religious) should wish for their children to be schooled separately from those who are being educated under the Comprehensive system, they should be required to pay for it without any subsidy from the state. If many of our private schools find that they need to close down as a result of these measures, the reply could be that they would still be welcome within the comprehensive fold, provided that their establishments had been kept in good order.

The concept of a fair society does certainly entail an attempt to eliminate unearned privilege from it, not only that which is exemplified by the purchase of special educational facilities by wealthy parents, but also the exercise of political power by hereditary right. If Britain is to maintain a bicameral parliamentary system, then it is fair that its hereditary basis should be removed[1]. Despite advocating that it had to be reformed, I still took up my seat in the pre-1999 House of Lords; but this was quite simply because I did not intend to exercise what would have amounted to a unilateral disarmament. It was, in my view, in the best interest of reformists that I exercised the unearned political power that I found in my hands.

The question now turns to what one might foresee as the future for the British (or any other) aristocracy, or indeed for the monarchy itself. I do naturally predict the removal of all political power from these institutions. If a role exists for them in the future, it is more liable to be concerned with the pageantry of tourism; for it will remain in the public interest that tourists should flock to our shores, to attend spectacular royal events, and to visit stately homes still populated by the individual families, proudly exercising their own concepts of pageantry within a long-established tradition of heredity. There is no reason to eliminate such behaviour, so long as the idea of inherited *political* privilege can be suppressed.

In the society of the future, we shall never attain (nor even wish to attain) equality. Complete uniformity would mean the death of individualism. People are not born equal, due to the diversity of their genetic codes. What we can aspire to attain, however, is equality of opportunity; and this implies that our children should emerge from the same educational system, in open competition for life's prizes, where the influence of nepotism, the old boy network, or such 'family' groups as are involved in freemasonry or the mafia, have been reduced to insignificance. Those who merit the top jobs will be enabled to rise to them by the excellence of their own performance in the field.

The meritocratic ideal will have been fulfilled when it is clear that no posts are being passed on from father to son without his suitability for such appointment being established in free competition against alternative applicants. The meritocrat will doubtless exercise more political power than the average man, but this is acceptable in that he has earned it and it is not transmissible to his progeny. His children will benefit from his excellence, not only from his wisdom perhaps, but also from the trappings of wealth which were at his disposal during his lifetime. But there will need to be a tightening up on the rules governing bequeathed wealth, if any true state of meritocracy is to be attained.

There is no contradiction in terms that we should promote the idea of a meritocracy in what we aspire to be an egalitarian society. Provided that the rise to high status stands as an open possibility for whomever might have the ability to reach such a goal, there is no breach of the egalitarian ideal. High expectations will be implicit within any democratic system where the principle of one man, one vote, is truly operative. The dream of unlimited opportunity may stand as the inspiration for any young person on the brink of his or her adult life. Its achievement will be all the more impressive when viewed in retrospect if it can be clearly established that it was attained against open competition at every step on the way.

---

[1] A regional basis might form one of the alternatives, but that still leaves open to debate the manner in which members should be appointed. (See relevant speeches in the Appendix, especially nos 4 and 7.)

6

Constraint and Freedom of Expression

Few of us at the outset of our lives are capable of perceiving much harm in the idea that we should be permitted to do what we wish. Some might describe this as personalised anarchic licence, but in the world we inhabit there are widespread expectations for freedom of choice and limitless opportunity; and denigrators of these are often the people who protest most vigorously when subjected themselves to regulation. It is only gradually that most of us wake up to the fact that constraints abound and that we depend upon them to protect ourselves against the incursions of others. In fact, in our present society and day and age, systems of constraint remain quite rigorous, in the respect that we still remove certain offenders from society to house them in penitentiary (or correctional) establishments. It is time that we should ask ourselves if this conforms with our ideal for social organisation.

We create a society which influences some individual members to offend against the law of the land. Their motive for doing so is often either piratical greed or a sense of revolt against the entire system. Many offenders see the system as promoting undeserving people to positions of affluence and power, while entrenching others there, at the expense of their own potential opportunity. Crime offers an alternative to blind acceptance of a system they to regard as being unfair from the start.

If the criminal stands guilty, so do we for the creation of this society which has failed his aspirations. We should therefore be reluctant to increase the degree of penalty so as to coerce the offender by deterrent force into an acceptance of a lifestyle which he has rejected. We should also be applying our investigative skill to identify the direction in which society might be altered so as to retain the loyalty and involvement of offending individuals, as well as identifying the best methods for re-educating them so that they begin to perceive this society which we are creating as one in which they can discover slots involving real opportunities for them.

The ideal should never be to incarcerate, but to oblige offenders to attend rehabilitation courses – provided of course, that it can be established that they are no longer a danger to the public. A system of open prisons would appear to be our best option, with psychiatrists rather than warders as the most suited to take charge. Once an offender is believed to have made a transition in attitude sufficient that he should be accepted as a potentially useful participant in society, then he should be freed from practically all custodial restraint.

Our biggest effort, however, should be to change society so that it becomes more attractive to young people from the start, inspiring them with a wish for fuller involvement. Much will depend upon the levels of constraint which are fixed upon recently released offenders, so that they can re-enter the social fold with their potential for rehabilitation unquestioned. We should be concerned to encourage and promote all manner of socially beneficial aspirations wherever the personal qualities for such achievement are in evidence. Special investigation should be made to discover where talent and ambition lie unseen. In a society where individualism is promoted, the range for potential development should be as wide as possible.

The ideal of individualism requires that there should be maximum freedom of expression for all members of society. But here again constraint of some kind becomes inevitable when particular individuals choose (for example) to distribute snuff films for the titillation of criminally unsympathetic sexual appetites or films of sadistic violence for the entertainment of our children. Prosecutions should be initiated on the grounds that such videos constitute an incitement to murder or to racial hatred perhaps. But it remains a delicate matter to discern when we might be justified in applying the heavy hand of censorship.

We are seldom able to take our moral stance over particular examples of behaviour on a basis of 'always or never'. Judgement requires application over a continuum of examples where subjective points of both tolerance and intolerance might be raised. The admissibility of advertisement is an appropriate case for consideration, with its requirement to establish when people should be constrained from attempting to persuade the rest of us to behave as they wish. An advertisement to murder might seldom be tolerated, but judgements can differ when one encourages us to smoke cigarettes to a point where our health is liable to be impaired. A majority view is all that we can really hope to establish on such an issue, which then promptly becomes political.

We find ourselves subject to far more behavioural constraints than is healthy for individualism. We are forbidden to drive above speed limits which even the police recommend being raised; we have for many decades been limited in the hours that we may drink alcohol in public places; we are still forbidden to partake of certain drugs which many psychologists regard as no more dangerous than alcohol; we are not allowed to seek the services of prostitutes in many a quarter they frequent; we are forbidden from participating in certain forms of sexual intercourse even with a consenting adult partner. In these non-victim areas, there is much that demands immediate reappraisal with a view to diminishing the levels of constraint.

The idea of there being a particular group of appointed individuals subjectively deciding what is good or healthy for the rest of us to adopt as our standard is abhorrent to my libertarian values. The direction of change required (currently pioneered in Holland) is to legalise as much as we dare and to regard what is done in the open as being that much easier to control. If people are to alter their habits, they should persuaded to do so via psychologically appropriate advertising campaigns – paid for by the imposition of taxes on the sale of such anti-social products as, for instance, cigarettes.

Wherever possible, government should encourage and promote the maximum variety of (innocuous) cultural activities within the territory it governs. The inspiration for these activities should be drawn from as wide a field of social, religious and ethnic variation as the region can exemplify. That will produce an environment in which individualism can best emerge and thrive. And that is the character of society which we should all be seeking to create.

7

The Wessex Regionalist Campaign

While at Oxford I was still uncertain as to where my ultimate political allegiance might lie. There could be no doubt where my own self-interest lay, as a landed aristocrat with a fair sum of capital already transferred to my name, in order that the family could survive the next batch of death duties; but I had been disgusted by the dearth of empathy which I had witnessed in many conversations where right-wing values prevailed. At the same time I had been alarmed by the venomous sentiments that I'd heard expressed concerning people of my kind, by both public and private figures who evidently had an axe to grind. I found it difficult to choose where I might really belong.

Back in the 1950s, there was still a feeling that the issue between the Left and the Right was on the score of whether the world was heading for a Communist or a Fascist world order. The Fascists had officially been routed during the recent World War, but I knew how (within my own family in effect) those ideals were still very much alive. My own sympathies lay in neither of those directions, because I detested totalitarian attitudes of any kind. They triggered memories of rigid intolerance in my own life; these instantly prompted me to identify with whatever opposition might prove possible under the circumstances.

I was in fact telling myself that my personal political ideals must lie within the traditional democratic fold. But the problem as I saw it was that democrats had never taken the trend of their own ideas to its logical conclusion. They might preach the concept of 'one man, one vote', but within the world order they were seeking to create – on the floor of the United Nations Assembly – this principle had lapsed. There were the big powers and the little powers; moreover, there was no way that a vote on the floor of the Assembly was going to determine the direction of world policy. That was a matter left to be sorted out behind closed doors, within secret enclaves of those privileged with access to power. Nor was there the slightest demand that each delegate at the United Nations should represent an approximately equal proportion of the human population.

This point of dissatisfaction with the existing formula for world democracy instigated my curiosity to discover a system that might function to implement more closely the democratic ideal – ergo, my attraction to the concept of 'one man, one vote' being translated on the international plane into 'one region, one vote'. I had seen that the current ideas of 'nationhood' were thwarting man's potential for evolving the democratic ideal towards its logical conclusion.

I was travelling a fair amount around Western Europe at the time and taking note how the countries demarcated on the European map were often comprised from smaller entities where an individual culture and lifestyle prevailed. The men of Saxony and Bavaria were utterly different species – as indeed were the people in Normandy and Provence, in Tuscany and Calabria, in Catalonia and Andalusia. But it was the distinctiveness between different regions in the Benelux group of countries, between Flanders and Wallonia for example, or between the north and south of Holland, which really brought my attention to the complexity of European diversity.

On returning to Britain, I observed how the whole issue of devolution was coming into focus for the first time this century, with both Scots and Welsh demanding autonomy. Devolution would certainly be a move in the right direction, I thought; but the nationalistic overtones of both the Scottish and Welsh also seemed dangerous from my standpoint. What was required was that all the regions of Britain should demand similar degrees of autonomy, with their loyalty switching from Westminster to the European Parliament, in the hopes that we might truly initiate a new political format for the Continent as a whole, in a United Regions of Europe.

When I presented myself as the Wessex Regionalist candidate for West Wiltshire in the general election of February 1974, I felt that I was making a significant stand, both for myself (this was the first occasion in my life when I had gone public to take a definitive political position) and for political theory as a whole, in that it brought into focus what the devolutionary logic really entailed. It didn't have to be a backward-looking movement, nostalgically hankering for the re-emergence of long past national status; it could instead be portrayed

The Wessex Regionalist Campaign

as the brightest case yet devised for nudging both Britain and Europe into the forefront of political relevance, in the evolution of democracy towards its ultimate global realisation.

I was content with the 521 votes I obtained. (No one had supposed for a second that I would avoid losing my deposit.) During the campaign I received many letters, some of them urging me to establish a Wessex Regionalist Party so that others could join in the fray. As a result, I was able to field seven candidates in the general election of 1979, which garnered a grand total of 3090 votes for the bunch of us; I also presented myself as the Wessex Regionalist candidate for the first Euro-election that same year – in a constituency which the authorities had (almost deferentially?) named as 'Wessex'. My own purpose in standing was to place the theory of government which I was advocating firmly within the European context, and I obtained 1706 votes for my efforts.

That was as far as I chose to take my Wessex Regionalist campaign. I did not want to become repetitive, by presenting myself as a candidate at all subsequent elections, with precisely the same message to deliver. I felt I could afford to pause awhile, and perhaps to seek new allies, before re-applying myself to the task of endeavouring to create, here in Europe, this prototype for a new world order.

8

Wessex Awake!

For the Wessex Regionalist general election campaign of 1979, I put out the following leaflet under the heading of 'Wessex Awake!'. It took the form of a 12-point programme.

WE DEMAND:

1: The same, and no less a degree of self-government for Wessex, as should be offered to Scotland – in an attempt to establish a federal pattern for the UK as a whole.

2: The creation of a Wessex Regional Assembly for the direction of our internal affairs, in place of county councils.

3: That the Wessex Assembly shall automatically receive a substantial proportion of all taxation revenue collected by the UK Parliament, to spend as the Assembly sees fit on regional responsibilities (e.g. employment, housing, transport, agriculture, fisheries, education, the health services, social welfare, law and order).

4: That the revenues from our mineral resources (including Dorset oil) be invested in the development of alternative energy sources, and in long-term regional employment opportunities – with an idea in mind for the ultimate self-sufficiency of Wessex, in terms of energy, nutrition, and all essential manufacture.

5: The introduction of a property tax, to be paid by any house buyer who has not worked or resided in Wessex for either seven years of his or her life, or for three consecutive years over the period immediately prior to the purchase.

6: The control of industrial expansion in Wessex to ensure ecological protection, and sympathy with the local environment. Also the encouragement of small businesses, craft industries, and community work projects, wherever they appear to be economically viable.

7: The promotion of Wessex as the political and economic ally of all other agricultural regions within Europe, to operate in defending common interests against their transformation by those regions which are more highly industrialised.

8: The planning of a Wessex-oriented transport system, to link up our principal cities, without having to depend solely upon routes directed towards London. There should be special emphasis upon an improved system of public transport.

9: The support of the various Wessex art councils and Wessex tourist boards, so as to encourage the growth of a regional identity and consciousness in the presentation of our region as a cultural whole.

10: The conservation of all that is best in our architectural heritage, with special attention paid to our cottages and villages. Also the protection and investigation of ancient sites.

11: The formation of a Wessex radio and television channel.

12: The promotion of a Wessex identity in sporting activities, on a par with Scotland, Wales and Ulster.

When it came to the Euro-election (also in 1979), the message I put forward in the local press and the speeches I was required to deliver was that the European Parliament should prepare itself for taking over many of the responsibilities at present exercised by various national assemblies. We should in fact anticipate and encourage a two way transference of power from Westminster, both upwards to the European Parliament and downwards to regional assemblies.

The net outcome should be that a region (such as Wessex) would control its own quality of life, whilst the more significant aspects of power – such as control of our economy, control of foreign policy and control of armed forces should be placed firmly under European direction. This would involve an end to sovereignty for what had formerly comprised the United Kingdom, with the MPs at Westminster finally legislating themselves out of a job[1]. Some would transfer to constituency representation within their particular region, while others would be elected to represent that region within the European Parliament.

We should not fear this loss of sovereignty, I argued: it was something which had in any case gradually been eroded over the years, and the time had come for us to identify more precisely which choices we needed to decide close to home and which to entrust to those in charge of the wider organisation of our welfare. It was important, for example, that the economy should be regulated centrally on a European basis, so that taxation could be levied uniformly throughout the Continent – modified by regional benefit schemes to ensure that the poorer regions had ample opportunity to improve their living standards until they matched those of the better-off regions. It was equally important that the regions should receive their established quota of the Continent's inland revenue *not* as an act of generosity from a central government but by statutory right on a per capita and per hectare basis – with different rates operating per-haps, according to whether a particular hectare was set to industrial, residential, agricultural or other specific usage.

The concept of government from Europe that I was advocating was very far from the idea of Britain's 'regions', which were then at the mercy of an omnipotent central bureaucracy, acting beyond our control. It was far more the fulfilment of the anarchist's dream of a central government with strictly limited and clearly demarcated areas of control. The real business of living (in the quality of life for its citizens) should be left for each of the regions to sort out as it might think fit, in all the variety that might best suit its individual inclination.

---

[1] This position may appear to conflict with one stated in a speech to the House of Lords (see page 77); however, the latter was made in consideration of the status quo still extant at the time.

Wessex Awake!

9

Wessex within a Federal Europe

When I stood as a 'Wessex Regionalist and European Federal Party' candidate in the Euro-election of 1979, I advocated a 24-point list of what was required for the well-being of 'Wessex within a Federal Europe' (as the leaflet was entitled). It read:

1: The Parliament at Strasbourg should furnish a political platform where the voice of Wessex can be expressed as participating within a Europe of Regions, rather than a Europe of Nations.

2: We should look forward to the emergence of a United Regions of Europe, that might be compared with the United States of America. Wessex will be one of these Regional States.

3: There should be a European Head of State: some much revered elder statesman, to be elected by the Parliament at Strasbourg.

4: All decisions of the European Supreme Court of Justice should be upheld and implemented by the authority of the European Parliament.

5: There should be a gradual transfer of sovereignty from Westminster to Strasbourg in three important spheres:
(a) the control of the armed forces
(b) the control of foreign policy decisions
(c) the control of the economy.

6: The supreme officers within the European High Command should be responsible to Strasbourg, with the entire British armed forces serving under this command.

7: Strasbourg must debate the foreign policies of all Western European nations, so that they can be fully co-ordinated.

8: There should be a European Foreign and Consular Service, responsible only to the Parliament at Strasbourg. This will replace the present national system.

9: Strasbourg must encourage European monetary union, with due regard to the transitional problems that this may involve for the weaker currencies.

10: The Parliament at Strasbourg must furnish Europe with a uniform tax structure (involving income tax, super tax and capital gains tax) applicable at the same levels within all European nations. This will not preclude the right of national or regional governments to raise taxes by additional methods, if they so choose.

11: Wessex and all other regions should receive a substantial tax rebate from such taxation revenue, apportioned in accordance with their per capita and per hectare rating as European Regions. This rebate should be spent as the regional assemblies see fit.

12: Another large portion of all federal taxation revenue should be paid annually into the regional fund at Strasbourg, with a view to effecting a gradual redistribution of capital and social resources over Western Europe at large.

13: A further portion of the federal taxation revenue should go into a European redevelopment fund, with a view to assisting those nations such as Britain with peculiar transitional problems, or generally assisting towards the cost of unifying the nations of our continent.

14: Applications should be made to the European Parliament to shoulder the cost (from out of this redevelopment fund) for changing the British road system from left to right.

15: The cost of linking Britain to France by several bridges and tunnels should also be financed from this fund.

16: The Common Agricultural Policy should be modified so as to ensure efficiency in farming, without destroying the idea that Europe should become agriculturally self-sufficient.

17: The representatives from Wessex should seek to ally themselves with the representatives of those European regions where farming is practised efficiently, asserting our mutual interests against regions where farming is practised inefficiently, or where the interests of agriculture as a whole are subordinated to industrial interests.

18: Strasbourg must co-ordinate and control the scientific and technological research of its member nations, so as to attain maximum efficiency and co-operation.

19: The operation of multinational companies in Europe should be carefully monitored, so as to avoid any upsurge of their influence to a degree that cannot be safely controlled by the elected representatives of the people.

20: Strasbourg must take charge of energy policy within Europe, which should be carefully planned to allow for the situation that will arise after our oil supplies have run out, involving heavy investment in alternative energy research.

21: Strasbourg must take general charge of environment policy, to ensure that national standards are consistently high.

22: The standardisation of weights and measurements according to the European metric system should be pressed forward to its conclusion.

23: A uniform electoral system of proportional representation, with single transferable vote, should be adopted by the Parliament at Strasbourg before the next Euro-elections.

24: Research should be undertaken at Strasbourg for a computerised voting system, for future adoption, whereby the voting strength of each delegate from a regional state is registered automatically within the European Parliament in direct relation to the number of people that the delegate's party can be shown to represent.

10

European Union

A United Regions of Europe is a goal that might just be obtainable within my lifetime; but one should not deceive oneself concerning the size of the obstacles along that path. It is only natural that the individual should fear the prospect of finding himself organised from a human grouping wider than the one to which he has previously become accustomed. And there is much over which the watchful individual should remain alert to ensure that this evolution is enacted without trespass on his established rights as the citizen of an autonomous region.

Some fear that, while other European nations are progressively regionalized, an economically dominant Germany will retain its territory intact and unified in its voting procedures as a measure of ensuring that its influence over the rest of Europe will emerge as unchallengeable. Its interests might then be enforced, overriding all opposition from other quarters, so that the other cities of Europe will have their status relegated under the imperial subjugation of Berlin.

This is an instance where I foresee the influence of the formerly British regions being asserted in defence of a truly democratic interpretation of the European constitution. The idea of Germany exercising a block vote to enforce Berlin's definition of European interests should not be tolerated, even if much political activity might be required to ensure that a free vote is always permitted on the floor of the European Parliament. Germany is as heterogeneously diverse as any of the other former nations of Europe, and the conflicting interests of agriculture versus industry, or of coastal regions versus those of the continental interior, can ultimately be exploited to ensure that rival lobbies will be filled with nationals who may previously have displayed a determination to vote together.

The most frequent doubt expressed concerning the viability of a united Europe, especially one that has been unified on the basis of its autonomous regions, concerns the recent example of the bloodshed in Yugoslavia. It is argued that regionalization must inevitably be equated with anarchy: that it throws one faction against the next, in a frantic effort to assert cultural dominance within a region that they both inhabit. If asked to choose between the proposals advocated for the division of Bosnia prior to the Dayton Accords, I would have opted for the one that approximated closest to the model I have in mind for a United Regions of Europe.

The terrible problems exemplified in the former Yugoslavia exercised man's diplomatic ingenuity to devise a solution that would bring the bloodshed to an end while at the same time respecting the justifiable expectations of all parties concerned. Ideally, within a United Regions of Europe all manner of minorities, where they constitute the majority within a population group that stands in excess of 500 thousand – which is admittedly an arbitrary figure – will have the right to determine the quality of life for that community, while respecting all divergences from their own cultural pattern that might exist within their own fold.

The principle of free cultural expression, no matter how small the minority in our midst, is fundamental to the spirit of regionalism, and steps should always be taken by a majority to ensure that such freedom endures. Rich diversity in the midst of any region both heightens and broadens its cultural scope. Tolerance is not only humane, but also rewarding. The idea of carving Bosnia, for example, up into ethnic partitions wherein the minority cultures could be expelled could hardly be endorsed in spirit, even if (as a pragmatic solution) it was the best that anyone could hope to implement at the time.

Shifting the example from Bosnia to Wessex, we might hypothesise the situation of a West Indian (or Pakistani) community finding itself in excess of the 500 thousand population mark and featuring as the majority within a certain district of (let us say) Bristol. It would have the right to set up its own institutions to control the quality of life within that district. This would not involve its secession from Wessex, but merely its right to regulate its own way of life, alongside that of all other communities in Wessex, and to find itself properly represented within the collective institutions of government.

Those in Western Europe who are inspired by the concept of a future United Regions of Europe should not despair from observing the fate of Bosnia and other parts of the former Yugoslavia. Terrible problems are perhaps even the necessary preliminary to inspirational solutions. Prompted by bloodshed in southeastern Europe, we must remain hopeful that Westerners will eventually feel moved to the sacrifices necessary to bring the former Soviet Bloc states into the same political fold as themselves, realizing that anarchy in the east of the Continent may spread to the west, unless the substance of our own relative stability, both in economic and political terms, can be offered in institutionalised form with an invitation that they should participate with us in this creation of a United Europe.

The nations of the EU should hurriedly evolve their own political union so that the old concept of nationhood is left firmly behind. We have the historical tradition and the economic muscle to devise a political umbrella beneath which all of our regional communities can thrive. From the example of how a United Regions of Europe can operate, inspiration will intensify in the nations of Central and Eastern Europe to accept the rules and the institutions which we have devised, and to accede for membership just as soon as we can allow.

11

World Government

Though I retain hope that a United Regions of Europe might be attained in my lifetime, the dream does not stop there; for the larger hope is that this prototype of polyglot cultural diversity within Europe can successfully be fused into a political whole that will inspire the rest of the world to develop a version of it as well. This evolution could be quite rapid, with the United Nations Organisation transforming itself into an Assembly of Equals for the implementation of a truly democratic world order.

In 1975 I wrote *A Regionalist Manifesto*, in which I tried to conceive of a form and manner in which the federated regions of the world might operate once this dream has been fulfilled. In brief, the principle was that our lives should be regulated at three different levels of political organisation: the quality of life at the regional level, economic life at the continental level, and the world's armed forces solely at the global level.

This would in effect be the fulfilment of the anarchist's ideal of non-interfering government at the top level, with as much individualism as possible encouraged down the line through a process of devolution. There would be a global Assembly of Equals whose principle function would be to guarantee a system where individual cultural groups could reign supreme in their own regions. Other functions for it would include the promotion and supervision of all major scientific research, the promotion of regional development schemes for under-developed regions, the provision of a world budget and the appointment of an international judiciary.

A few words are required on the subject of a world budget. This would need to be financed from an annual world welfare tax, with each continental group of nations contributing substantially in proportion to the world government's assessment of their gross national product – a figure which, after gradual increase, would be liable to reach a proportion of about 25% of GNP. The continental groups of regions would each be responsible for the collection of these dues; in the event of defaulting payments, the sum would be collected by armed force, as a last resort, if necessary.

On the question of representation and procedure, a minimum population should be established for any regional state to qualify for representation within the Assembly of Equals. The ambassadors who sit in that body should do so by the right of annual election from the regional assembly which they represent; nor should there be more than one ambassador from each state, however large it might be; and this ambassador should cast his single vote independently from all other ambassadors. All decisions on the floor of the Assembly should be taken by majority vote; all proceedings within it should be open to public view.

While I recognise that there is liable to be considerable variation in size of populations between the different regions, we should still give some thought to the optimum; and the logic on this question might run as follows. The Assembly of Equals should contain less than 1,000 ambassadors, with 500 as the suggested optimum. By the time of this writing, world population will probably have passed the 5 thousand million mark; so the optimum size for any regional state can therefore be calculated by dividing 5 thousand million by 500, which gives us 10 million. For the purposes of greater flexibility, we might fix this somewhere between 5 and 15 million.

Regions with a population of less than 5 million would still have the right to insist that they stand in control of their own quality of life; but in terms of representation elsewhere, such a region would need to negotiate shared representation either with a neighbour or with a group of such small regions which had fallen short of the 5 million mark in the established size of their respective populations. In the case of states with a population in excess of 15 million, they would doubtless eventually come to see that it was in their best interest to think in terms of sub-division into regional states, so as to acquire greater voting strength on the floor of the Assembly of Equals. But they should be under no compulsion to sub-divide, unless some constituent portion of that state should apply for separate representation.

A crucial question arises as to where this Assembly of Equals should be situated, with its implication of the site emerging as a

World Government

future world capital. Various considerations need to be borne in mind over this issue, not least the fact that it will only come to the forefront of human concern (at the earliest) around the turn of the 22nd century. We should also appreciate that, in tomorrow's world, technological achievement will have evolved so far that such matters as the regulation of a building's air-conditioning, irrigation and even climatic control will be easily within reach. It is already possible to tackle such tasks as the transformation of desert into garden. So the consideration of an ideal site for world government is far wider than it might have been even a few decades back in the 20th century.

Thus it should give grounds for less surprise that I put forward the suggestion that the ultimate siting for our world capital ought to be the Sinai peninsula – a region, currently so sparsely populated, which Egypt might permit to being fully internationalised and given over to these purposes, for the sheer prestige of having world government situated on its doorstep. The rest of us will be able to rejoice in the fact that the central organisation for our global civilisation will have returned approximately to the point where it originally came into first bloom – a site which might also be judged as lying at the pin-point centre of our planet's geographical spread of land; the natural nexus for global communications.

I shall venture to predict that the year in which this World Government comes into effective operation will be designated by all the regional (and national) governments as the year 0001 of the new era of World Government, as it may become known. The years in which we are currently living will then be described as BWG, or Before World Government, as opposed to being AWG, or After World Government. That should be sufficient, until such time as we are in effective communication with extra-terrestrial governments existing elsewhere within our universe, at which point a further age (or ages) will no doubt need to be initiated.

12

Individualism, Catastrophe and Terrorism

With the advent of World Government, the arena will exist for humanity to examine and debate the problems arising from abuse of the earth's environment. It is then perhaps that individualism might get identified as the big evil. This is because the individual often puts his own interests before those of the common good, without fully perceiving how his endeavours may be contributing to some particular global catastrophe. The World Government Assembly will be an arena where such problems will get exposed and rectified, with attention to matters both great and small. The Government will furnish a structure wherein grandeur of scale will produce maximum economy of effort, without losing sight and interest in smallness of scale, where the solution of problems assumes the character of personal endeavour and where the interest of the individual can more easily be sustained.

Delay in the world's attention to the ecological issues which in the long run might threaten man's future will result in their increase, creating a greater public awareness after the incidence of predicted catastrophic events. These will disrupt our lives until there is a sufficient demand for action to ensure that the subjects get debated and resolved in accordance with solutions recommended by the majority. The concern of World Government will be to minimise the effect of catastrophes on the human race, no matter what they might be. I could mention the (rare, but inevitable) calculation that our planet will find itself on a collision course with other celestial bodies. It would be the responsibility of World Government to discover a scientific means to divert such objects from our path – by means of a strike from a fleet of rockets with nuclear warheads, or whatever. Catastrophes are part of the natural order. But our ability to discern when and where they may be inflicted upon us will improve greatly over the years, enabling us to take evasive or preventive actions to diminish the consequences.

We must also, of course, continue to concern ourselves over the way individuals create catastrophes with political or even criminal deliberation – where a minority, say, seeks to oblige the majority to give way under pressure from threats, or the enactment of such threats, to the implementation of demands. In its simplest form this might be a case where innocent hostages get taken, and perhaps even executed, if money (or whatever) does not get paid. It would seem that, in this technological age, such methods are becoming common-place and ever more drastic in their nature. There have been cases of extortion where particular criminals have held a chain of superstores to ransom, on the threat to contaminate their products in a way that might involve indiscriminate loss of life amongst their customers. Worse, the possibility now exists for a single criminal to organise the theft or acquisition of some nuclear device, with the threat to explode it at a site of dense human habitation. Nerve gases have already been released in the ventilation systems of a capital city's public services. We may anticipate at some point in future the contamination of metropolitan reservoirs with a deadly virus, coupled perhaps with the instigation of sudden cybernetic chaos.

On each such occasion, those in authority will have to consider the extent to which a minority can be permitted to hold the majority to ransom. Should they submit to the demand in question, encouraging thereby other minorities to seek implementation of their wishes by similar methods? In the long run, such impositions of a minority's will cannot be tolerated, and the suppression of such terrorism will become increasingly a matter of concern for World Government, if it has not already been tackled on the regional or continental levels. This will lead no doubt to the creation of a supreme anti-terrorist intelligence service and strike force, under the international control of the World Government.

A usual source of discontent in any society has to do with the sustenance or creation of more egalitarian conditions. Confrontation continues between haves and have-nots concerning the ownership and expropriation of the world's resources and amenities. A special danger exists if a perception of injustice in this area develops in ideological linkage to one of the world's religions. The Islamic world, for example, could choose to exploit such a sense of injustice in order to attract whole populations to its faith. Alternatively, or concurrently, groups of terrorists may emerge to make threats on this basis while receiving shelter in difficult Islamic terrain, such as recently has been the case in Afghanistan. Here again it will be for the World Government's international strike force to assume responsibility for eliminating the threats.

Such solutions will prove impermanent, however, if the global problem of inequality remains unattended to. There will always be individuals to remind us of the issue, offering ideas perhaps which might lead to the creation of cults advocating alternative purposes in life to the accepted norm. Such cults might also resort to terrorist strikes, to try to oblige others to rearrange society as they see fit. The one and only long term solution is the creation of a fair society, where the difference and distinction between individuals can be explained on a basis that displays true empathy for the have-nots. It will be the responsibility of World Government to pronounce and preach this attitude, and to produce conditions wherein the world's resources furnish greater benefit for every one of us. The option of identifying with fringe groups where individualistic terrorism is recommended then loses its appeal, with society becoming safer in consequence.

Individualism is an essential ingredient to a fair society. At the same time, we must remain cognisant of the fact that, if the individual becomes excessively egocentric (or even selfish), then individualism as a credo will result in genuine anarchy. Restraint does need to be exercised somewhere along the line, for we must not permit minorities to dictate to us what they personally might regard as the conditions best suited for the welfare of the majority. A system needs to exist in which society both nurtures the individual and restrains him as the need arises, in accordance with the established will of the majority. Within such a political framework we may perceive our best hopes for a socially co-operative future.

13

Warfare and Punishment

Society will always have to contend with instances where the group personality of entire regions poses a threat to the rest of us. It is the same danger which is evident, on a smaller scale, when particular individuals band together, acting in concert or even alone, for the exploitation of society for their own ends. In both cases we are talking about trends which need to be reversed, either by military action or by punishment.

The will of the majority is always vulnerable if a mechanism is not in place to arrest and reverse the actions taken as a result of a minority's aggression. This may be countered by a region's capacity to muster sufficient armed force (under licence from the World Government) to arrest and prosecute those who are pursuing group interests in disregard of what has been pronounced the common good. In serious cases, it may become the responsibility of the World Government to bring the situation under control.

If it is decided by the will of the majority that the actions of some particular region are working towards the destruction of the existing world governmental system, then in the last resort warfare has to be threatened. With all the refinement of diplomatic techniques, this threat should take the form of suggestion as to what might occur if the other side does not choose to climb down, along with anti-terrorist activities in evidence within the major cities of the insurgent territory. If the World Government is to be in a position to enforce its decisions by armed force where necessary, the quality of its armaments and of its training must be second to none.

The whole nature of warfare will doubtless be different from what we know today. We should anticipate that the other side will avail itself of all manner of ruthless terrorist outrage, either threatened or perpetrated within our home territory – this against a backdrop of life continuing as normal, up to the moment of its happening, with a persistent flow of professedly non-political tourists criss-crossing the frontiers. Front line troops may well be disavowed by the combatant groups, due to the clandestine nature of their operations. But the World Government's regular armed forces must also be there on the ready, for use as the ultimate heavy strike force if required.

We need also to be concerned with the reversal of trends where individual criminals are concerned. There will always be occasions, even within a fair society, when punishment needs to be inflicted on those who are breaking rules agreed on by the majority; but we should always be clear about our theoretical justifications. Punishment for the sake of retribution cannot be justified in a society where empathy prevails. Our ability to identify with a wrongdoer and comprehend his motivation should preclude any sentiment that he be made to experience a fate similar to his victim's, because we are able to see in him the personification of what we ourselves might have been like had our genetic structure or upbringing been different. The deterrent motivation for punishment comes into focus most especially at times when law and order is breaking down; but whilst we may empathise with the idea of deterrence in that it may enhance our possibilities for self-preservation, we should remain aware that, on a broader scale, maltreatment of criminals merely reinforces the divide between *them* and *us* to an extent that punishment of any kind gets perceived as society's rejection of them for our own selfish reasons.

A more unified world society will emerge if we adopt the corrective approach to punishment. The wrongdoer is taken into custody – preferably only open custody – while his behaviour is studied by appropriate medical experts, so that he can be persuaded by use of social therapies to mend his ways, earning his release just as soon as we can convince ourselves that he is no longer a danger. There should be no crime regarded as too abominable to warrant permanent exclusion from re-entry into the common fold. On the other hand even mild offenders, if it is judged that they still represent a danger, should in some instances be segregated from the rest of us – albeit under humane conditions, and with the possibility for re-classification never too distant in time.

Much study should be made as to the best ways of reintegrating criminals within the society they have formerly rejected. Systems should emphasise the concept of rewards for improved behaviour far more than penalties for undesirable behaviour. The expense of rehabilitation will be less in the long run than that of letting criminals loose on society un-rehabilitated. Ideally, rehabilitation should be a service which continues long after it has initially been established, to minimise the possibility for subsequent relapse.

If continuing rehabilitation programmes are regarded as intrusive into the lives of former criminals, the line has to be taken that punishment *does* entail a loss of individual rights until such a time the criminal's current behaviour warrants their full restitution. The rights of man are conditional on his cooperation with the rest of society. In the event of continuing non-cooperation, a criminal should, in the last resort, be given the choice of continued exclusion from the rest of society or instant reintegration with the rest of society after his behaviour has responded to some more drastic treatment, such as lobotomy or castration. These last two are, of course, extreme solutions which should never be forced on a criminal without his considered assent.

The society which can learn to take its wrongdoers back into its embrace displays an attitude where more universal integration becomes a possibility, whereas the chastisement of criminals merely reinforces their concept of *them* and *us*. A spirit of unity finally generates its own rewards, including that of a sharp decrease in social paranoia. It is when paranoia gets encouraged and ever more deeply rooted in our attitudes towards one another that people start perceiving the rest of the world as enemies. A psychological atmosphere then exists for fractious discord and an inclination towards the outbreak of criminal violence or even war.

The civilisation which can educate itself to produce socially conscious citizens within socially conscious political organisations is one where the problems of paranoid antagonisms are least likely to emerge. But this will only obtain where government has learned to empathise with the position of those governed and where the individual can identify with the benevolent intent of those who govern.

14

A Charter for World Government

At the time when a majority of the world's political regimes agree that it is in their mutual self-interest to transform such international institutions for government as may already exist into something more specifically organised for the purposes of world government – such as the United Nations Organisation of today – it will then be necessary to determine the precise format for the new institutions and the constitution under which they should operate. A special committee should be created to advise the assembled ambassadors on the implications of all possible choices, with particular recommendations concerning the form they should choose; we should anticipate that there will then ensue global elections to determine whom should represent each region. The first task for the ambassadors to undertake would be the compilation and signing of a Charter for World Government, which would then serve as the authority by which all subsequent decisions were enacted into law. I suggest that this charter might read:

WE THE REPRESENTATIVES of the political regions on this planet, willingly establish the authority of The Assembly of Equals to determine and enact the rules by which our individual societies shall relate to one another in a spirit of economic and cultural co-operation and encouragement, and the methods by which these decisions shall be enforced. These powers are offered in the expectation that the aforesaid Assembly shall protect and promote the best interests of the individuals thus governed, with a view to enabling them to correlate with one another in self-esteem and the attainment of peace of mind. They shall be listed as follows:

The Assembly will debate and openly establish the values that should underlie the workings of World Government and on the matter of which goals should be given priority over others, within the provision of assistance to attain such ends.

The Assembly shall at all times respect the unique quality of all individuals and the differences in character between them, in respect for the principles of individualism.

The Assembly shall at all times respect the differences in culture between regions, without intruding upon their right to stand in control of their own quality of life.

The Assembly shall create and then facilitate the operation of global communication, so as to create a universal cultural umbrella beneath which the individual regions of this planet may discover and retain their personal conception of identity.

The Assembly shall bear in mind, and propagate where possible, the emergence of a fair world society.

The Assembly shall assume a readiness for extra-terrestrial civilisations to make contact with our own, in preparation for the creation of a galactic society, which recognises the ultimate unity of this universe and is prepared to revere that unity as being of supreme importance to each individual's innermost nature.

Once this charter has been signed by the representatives from all (or at least a two-thirds majority) of the regions on this planet, the next essential task will be the reorganisation of the world's political infrastructure.

15

The Rights of the Individual Man

The rights of man have been long debated, but even more so since libertarian values started to prevail. These rights are sometimes perceived as the antithesis of governmental rights, even perhaps as a hindrance to efficient government. They are also suspect for the qualifications that may need to be understood, if not actually listed, for their implementation in practice. These do need to be stated.

Normally it is government which takes the initiative in laying down the rules concerning any electoral contest; but at least in Britain, government has traditionally been wary of furnishing the individual with his most natural defence against the abuses of government, in the form of a legislated list of his rights. The new Labour Goverment of 1997 began introducing such legislation, after having in opposition won electoral advantage by proposing it; meanwhile, the European Parliament had for some time been outflanking the national parliament on this matter, obtaining kudos by pursuing these goals over its head. One way or the other, we now stand on the brink of a new era in regard to human rights, not only in Britain but worldwide; and it remains the concern of writers – perhaps even more than that of politicians – to review what should feature on the list.

My particular concern is to ensure that the individual is protected from society at large against the threat of being coerced into conformity. Government has its hands sufficiently full with the requirements of regulating the economy, maintaining law and order and conducting a nation's foreign policy without inviting frontal assault from individualists on the question of unlegislated rights. Whatever final form they may take, these rights are now at hand; and there should be no question of slackening in our pressure upon government to recognise them.

From my own perspective, I have long stood in hope that the following rights of the individual should ultimately be recognised in the form of a legislated charter – although the precise age at which the human embryo, infant, child or even adolescent might be attributed with some, or any, of them remains open to further debate.

1: The right to life, provided that my behaviour does not constitute an immediate threat to the lives of other people.

2: The right to do whatsoever I please with my body, to the point of terminating all life within it, if I so choose.

3: The right to establish (and to embellish) my own lifestyle, provided that it is not injurious to other people.

4: The right to privacy within such a lifestyle, provided that I am conducting it in compliance with common law.

5: The right to property, in terms of land or material possessions, whose usage is at my choice, provided that this does not conflict with the established will of the majority.

6: The right to choose for my personal association whatever family form might suit me the best.

7: The right to equality in opportunity, until the point has been reached when my individual abilities can be assessed for their particular merit.

8: The right to employment suitable to my abilities, if necessary from the hands of the state.

9: The right to offer my services for employment wherever work is available.

10: The right to protection and welfare benefits from the hands of the state, for myself and my dependants, according to the established rules for such welfare distribution.

11: The right to protection from physical or psychological coercion, from other members of the public or from the officials of state.

12: The right of access to official files of information on my life and personality.

13: The right to the same treatment as anyone else, in the eyes of the law.

14: The right to trial when accused of breaking the law, and the assumption of innocence, until my guilt has been satisfactorily proven.

15: The right to proclaim and to publish whatever viewpoints I might hold, provided that they do not transgress the essential rights of others.

16: The right to associate with whomever I please, and to organise their gatherings for the purpose of discussion or peaceful demonstration.

17: The right to select whatever candidate I might choose, to represent me in the political arena.

18: The right to present myself for election, as an alternative to the existing government, and to strive legally to win support for my candidature.

19: The right to govern, if I can win the support of the majority in such an election, for as long as that majority holds.

20: The right to worship in whatever temple I might please, in free association with other people of a similar creed.

21: The right to prosecute any individual, or institution, who seeks to suppress these rights.

The acceptance by government of a given list of rights for the individual man is no guarantee that our quality of life will improve thereafter. History has featured many authoritarian paternalistic regimes which have had no respect for the rights of man and in which absence of individual freedom of choice is judged an acceptable price to pay for established social welfare. The argument is also put forth that, with such a list fully operative, the state's welfare might gradually be eroded and then destroyed.

The case for establishing such a list is that we need to be protected from situations of extreme adversity, and we must always have the means at our disposal to change our government whenever that appears to be the desirable remedy for our ills. The recognition of our rights acts as a shield from behind which a political campaign can be conducted in the expectation of fair play. It places the individual when in opposition to government almost upon a level footing with the powers-that-be. Only with such guarantees can the conditions remain assured that society will always be able to make a free choice concerning those who should govern it.

16

Marital Prospects

When I was a boy I certainly imagined that I would make someone a faithful husband and that I would find myself an adoring wife to love and cherish for the rest of my days. Then as an adolescent when conversation on these subjects became more intense and idealised, the concept of virginity entered the picture. This probably was linked to some macho notion of loss of face in being seen to take second hand goods in marriage when many another man was thought to obtain them first hand. It would relegate one to the derided status of being a second class male if one had talked (at that age) of the likelihood of finally pairing up with a sexually experienced girl.

Over the question of male premarital conduct, it was clear that dual standards prevailed. I did not expect to be a virgin at the time of meeting whomever was to become my future wife; and I knew perfectly well that it was not expected of me within the particular social stratum in which I had been raised, where young men were generally expected to 'sow their wild oats', even if disposed towards fidelity in subsequent marriage. I found this clearly indicated by virtually all the girls that I first dated. They had been told by their parents to anticipate there would have been some libertine experimentation in the lifestyles of their young escorts. They were merely concerned that it shouldn't continue after a suitable degree of intimacy had been established with them.

My earliest sex life followed what was regarded in these circles as nothing out of the ordinary – which is to say that I indulged in a fair amount of homosexual games prior to the age of puberty (thoroughly sensual, but discretion forbids me to recount too much of that). Then while at Eton, I was accused erroneously of having a relationship with a boy older than myself, whom I only knew by sight and not even by name until after the scandal had broken. The humiliation of such public 'exposure' traumatised me against the prospect of having homosexual intercourse with anyone ever again. I resolved at that point that, no matter what other sexual fields I might decide to pioneer in, I'd leave such endeavours to others, who might perhaps (but not necessarily) be better fitted for it.

I was a slow starter when it came to any real heterosexual fulfilment. Having failed to lose my virginity at the age of 17 on a trip to the South of France which had been intended for that purpose, I fared rather better (at a price) once I was doing my National Service in the Life Guards; but I was 19 by then, and it was still a couple of years before I was indulging in love relationships. Even then there was a problem in that I was deferential to their insistence that the hymen (that symbol of devout virginity) should remain intact, which of course created huge barriers preventing me from any sense of true fulfilment in such intercourse.

When the time finally came that I was copulating with a girlfriend in the manner for which our bodies had been evolved, I was labouring at a disadvantage; for these girlfriends had never been treated with the same deference that I had previously given to others. So I was entering the relationships as the more inexperienced partner, which was somehow damaging to my male self-esteem. I had to accept it of course, but it made me feel uncomfortable.

That brings me to the stage when I endeavoured to rethink my whole attitude to life – the period of my relative reclusion after coming down from Oxford. I was trying to determine the conditions in a relationship with any girl that might enable me to feel psychologically comfortable. I saw that I was going to have to accept that the girls of any interest I met were now always liable to have had wider experience than myself. I was once given advice by someone considerably older, whom I respected, that it was just a question of driving myself to catch up on their total of love affairs; but this wasn't as easy as he'd made it sound. I was becoming inhibited in my efforts to seduce because I feared that my relative inexperience would immediately be perceived.

Eventually I found myself formulating a solution, which came closer than anything previously to furnishing me with a means to placing myself on a level of equality with the women I might hope to seduce. All right, I could accept their wider knowledge of sexual relationships; but I wouldn't give myself quite so wholeheartedly to the spiritual blend. I would do my best to become all that was expected of me in terms of the personality they were hoping to find in me, not from any act of falsehood on my part, but simply from a concern to be of value to that person. On the other hand there was perhaps now a part of me that I was concerned to keep in reserve – someone who might be described as standing just behind the scene and observing all that was going on.

This 'Me' in reserve could afford to develop more than one relationship at a time, endeavouring in each to become the person that my partner might want me to be and essentially to become of real value to her, while taking pleasure in the fact that this was so. I could afford to conduct several of these relationships simultaneously – not secretively, for I was already endeavouring to live by the rule of 'candour'. And the more such relationships I could effectively keep going within a state of mutually stimulating value, the more I could dismiss from my mind the relative disadvantage in experience which might have troubled me at the outset.

I was in fact discovering that I had a penchant for polygyny. I began to feel more secure in such relationships. What remained to be seen however, was whether I could hold the women whom I had initially attracted on this ticket; and there were to be many failures before I could claim that I was getting anywhere at all with such novel ideology.

17

The Polymorphous Society

For too long has it been the accepted goal in Western civilisation that a single man and a single woman shall unite in holy wedlock, to raise a brood of children – the wife acting essentially as the nest-builder, with her husband as the (hunter-gatherer cum) breadwinner for her individual family unit. This still represents the cultural expectation for most of us, although we are quick to admit that in practice it frequently no longer works out like that. The nuclear family is transforming into something amorphous. We can count amongst our friends and neighbours many a single parent. There is still a considerable number which pays more than lip service to its marital vow of fidelity in monogamous life-partnership. But there are others who now think far more in terms of serial monogamy, or at any rate of marital cheating, wherein the original formula is significantly undermined. Then come the overt polygynists and the polyandrists, and even the group-marital participants, who sometimes quite flagrantly flout the cultural expectations of the rest of society.

The solution in some people's eyes is to put over the message in ever stronger terms that the nuclear family consists of a monogamous couple, rearing their brood of children with a little help from the state. As the statistics for aberration from this narrow path of monogamous wedlock increase, so does the shrillness of the cries from moralists that more drastic steps should be taken to shepherd people back into the time-honoured practices.

This is a mistaken approach, which is unlikely to yield significant results. The current variety of choice available when Europeans come to select the family form to best suit their individual requirements is a part of the liberalisation in values which started as a result of the social upheaval from two world wars. It also results from the diminution in significance of a man's traditional role as breadwinner for his family, with that role already partially transferred into the hands of the welfare state – plus the attention that may now be given to a woman's preferences concerning such questions of family lifestyle.

In my view we are reaching a point in social evolution where the law will need to be changed – at the European level, if our regional assemblies are not yet functioning by then. Our legislators should cease their endeavours to prop up the monogamous family unit at the expense of others and concern themselves instead with the relationship between mother and child, no matter what the marital bonding she may (or may not) have chosen for herself. That is where the future stability of society can be doctored to its improved welfare. Parliament should legislate to ensure that a mother has all that she might require for the upbringing of her children – food, housing, clothing, schooling, medicare and social counselling – free of charge and without heavy questioning concerning the nature of the family form she may have chosen to adopt.

The day that Parliament legislates to make it illegal for the officials of state to make public record of a mother's marital (or non-marital) status will perhaps mark the initiation of the polymorphous society. Monogamous society is becoming a thing of the past, and it will eventually be recognised that the marital format for our emergent society is multi-faceted or 'many-shaped'. I am not suggesting that Parliament should ever be concerned to legislate, with deliberation, in order to make things easier for the serial monogamists, or for the polygynists and polyandrists in our midst. But it should feel obliged to remove the stigma of illegitimacy from any child: a stigma that was placed there because of how the parents chose to behave, rather than as a result of any fault attributable to the child himself.

These suggestions will no doubt entail a significant increase to the running cost of our welfare state, with a consequently heavier burden upon the shoulders of the taxpayer. But I would contend that, once this system is fully operative, the taxpayer may expect to break even on his ultimate cost of living. What he pays out in higher taxes, he will recuperate in terms of the saving in family expenditure which formerly had to come from out of the breadwinner's earnings. Subsidised rent, or even direct grant, for the housing of children and for their clothing, in addition to all other back-up services, will reduce the cost to every parent. People will finally insist that our welfare state should recognise its responsibilities in these matters, rather than spend time and money in the unrewarding endeavour to fix that responsibility upon the shoulders of errant fathers and the like.

If it is protested that some of us might regard it as unfair that our contributions to the Inland Revenue should support the children of others when we ourselves have opted for a bachelor or spinster lifestyle, then I would point out that all have advantages to gain from our welfare state – not least in its provision for a thriving younger generation, raised in fine health by these methods, which will perform services to sustain all taxpayers through ill health or old age. I am envisioning a system where we all take good care of one another, in the knowledge that our own special needs will be addressed by others whom our taxes once supported.

The polymorphous society may be moving up on us faster than we imagine. Its individual members, both men and women, have new roles in their service to it not yet properly identified. While women may be emerging as the victors in their control of the family, with all probability of its ultimate culmination in matrilineal descent, I would still speculate upon men retaining their pre-eminence as function- aries of the state – partly due to their diminishing obsession over the family. So both genders may congratulate themselves upon having dominant roles to play within the new order.

18

Pioneering as a Polygynist

I had identified my personal inclinations as being of a polygynous nature. I had also convinced myself that European culture was gradually switching over from being a monogamous society to a polymorphous society, where the emphasis in effect would be for the mother, not the father, to select whatever family form might suit her the best. Despite the fact that I was a mere man, my pioneering instinct came into play, urging me to channel my sex life into fronting that evolution. I do happen to be temperamentally suited to such a role. The requirement of a pioneer is to be bold enough to enjoy the dangers involved in the exploit, while having worked towards a vividly imaginative understanding of the unknown territory that requires to be explored. I believed myself to be the right person for such a task.

My first public statement denoting rejection of the official marital formula came in 1966 when I announced that I was having 'an anti-marriage' with the young woman with whom I was currently living. It wasn't intended as a significant pronouncement, but the tabloids had been badgering me to declare whether marriage was intended in this relationship, so in a spirit of exasperation I finally pronounced that we were getting anti-married; and the phrase got slotted into some journalists' jargon for the sixties – to which they added the phrase an anti-divorce when the woman announced that she was leaving me. (We are still excellent friends!)

The concept of it having been an anti-marriage was perhaps misplaced. I knew from the start that I would always need to marry properly one day, if I should wish that any son of mine would ever enjoy the Longleat inheritance, which happens to be entailed upon the marquisate. There was no manner for me to have a son and heir who would (after my decease) become the 8th Marquess of Bath without him being able to produce the necessary documents to prove that his mother and I had been legally married at the time of his birth. So a legal marriage with someone or other had always been intended since I ever first gave thought to the subject.

There was one particular girlfriend, Anna, who had occasionally been coming to stay with me, or to travel abroad with me, since the time when I had been at art school in Paris, back in 1959. She had been a mere schoolgirl at the time but had lived with me in the studio I was renting in the Rue de la Grande Chaumière. In the sixties she had met and married someone else, although her visits to Longleat had continued over the period. At the time when she was contemplating a divorce, in 1968, it was weighing heavily on me that, at the age of 36, I had yet to produce a son and heir. What inhibited me, however, was that I still aspired to build up a family on polygynous lines, with many wives and many children from each of them. So it was important that, before I took that dreaded step into official wedlock, my future wife should clearly understand and accept my intentions.

As my solicitor explained to me, signed agreements have little relevance if you are seeking to rearrange and reinterpret the prevalent institution of marriage – or not if a divorce were ever under consideration. But I did draw up a written list of points that were verbally agreed between Anna and myself, concerning the nature of the marital union on which we were considering embarking. The list may have been more concerned with questions of property rights, but it was certainly also agreed that she accepted my polygynous intents, provided (admittedly) that I would leave her to decide in her own time and way whether she might wish to participate actively in whatever polygynous practices I might bring to fruition. She did indicate that she thought she might be amenable to participation once she felt secure in the marriage and tenure of the manorial responsibilities.

As soon as we had a child on the way, I married Anna. The baby turned out to be a beautiful and delightful girl; we had to wait an additional five years before acquiring the intended son and heir. In the meantime I continued with the task of accumulating my family group of lady friends, whom I always hoped to persuade to have children by me, though in practice they merely toyed with the idea, since they remained dubious concerning what the fate of such children might be.

As time progressed some of these relationships proved long-standing, and the question arose as to the correct word to describe our degree of intimacy and togetherness. Legally speaking, they weren't my wives; nor would my wife have settled for them being allotted that description. But if I had started talking about my concubines or mistresses, it might have been regarded by some as disparagement. So we settled eventually for the humorous and affectionate term of 'wifelet', from which of course it followed suit that I must be one of their 'hublets'.

I do now have a love-child by one of them, although I feel obliged to respect her wishes for me to refrain from revealing their names or whereabouts. But I can at least regard this as a belated start to my greater familial intentions. Thus I may yet be able to demonstrate, by example, how the polygynous family unit is just as valid as its monogamous counterpart for the upbringing of a healthy (socially positive and culturally catalytic) brood of children within our European civilisation. At the age of 68, there might still be time!

19

Preaching by Example

Ihave already described how I am endeavouring to preach the message of variety within an emergent polymorphous society by actually creating a polygynous family in its midst. I regard the technique of preaching by example as one that is well suited to my temperament. It is perhaps the most effective of all methods in persuasive discussion to produce the example of what you are contending should exist and suggest that it might now be regarded as a model for others to imitate.

Nor is it solely within the domain of family morality that I am seeking to employ the technique. I have been striving for years to play my (infinitesimally small) part in the re-emergence of Wessex upon the world's atlas. Coaxing the population where I live to start thinking of themselves as Wessaxons, rather than as Englishmen, is half the battle, yet not one where it can really be claimed that I have made any significant progress to date.

But the pressure for change along this particular evolutionary path is being applied from political quarters too. Politicians are growing aware how their constituents increasingly resent the distance that is opening up between the governors and the governed. There is a premium to be won by bringing government back closer to the people, which stands in partial explanation for the recurrent interest in devolution. Eventually we may anticipate that the issue will be seen as ripe enough for full political realisation.

At the point when this occurs, I would hope that my own groundwork on the resurrection of a Wessex identity might finally be appreciated; and I would regard the re-emergence of Wessex upon the political map of Europe as another case of my preaching by example. For with Wessex actually there in existence, I could make much more of an argument for rapid progress towards the creation of a United Regions of Europe as an umbrella organisation for a multiplicity of individual regions practising their own distinctive culture, beneath an umbrella of economic security to which all such cultures make their invaluable contributions.

This would be a Europe which contained a fully regionalized Yugoslavia, Romania and Poland, although the destiny of Russia perhaps remains more ambiguous. (It is notable how the former Russian empire has been subjected to regionalization from within; the Russian Federation itself might splinter further, with different regions acquiring new associative allegiance, either to the west or to the south.) Once the example of the United Regions of Europe existed, then there would be other parts of the globe which would follow suit and organise themselves upon similar lines – partly for their economic well-being and partly for the attainment of political clout where international politics is concerned.

If that summarises my endeavour to preach politics by example, it leads on to the question of how I might preach pantheism while employing the same technique. The answer lies perhaps in the existence of my autobiography, which goes by the name of *Strictly Private*. This already consists of some four million words, spread out over 14 books, and the tale has only just reached the 1980s. In ten years from now, I might just about have brought my life's tale up to the date of my current existence. My ambition, of course, is that it will be the best autobiography that has ever been written – to be found on my internet website at www.lordbath.co.uk.

The task I have set myself is a mammoth one, but I am setting on record the example of someone who has worked out for himself the pantheistic *modus operandi*, along with the principles, values and underlying logic of such a faith. Whatever problems have emerged in my life, I discuss in the minutest detail within the autobiography until I feel that I am edging them towards their resolution. I create thus a platform on which I feel as if I might have something of consequence to proclaim. I like to imagine too that the commentary is entertaining in its own right, so that the work will eventually come to the attention of a cult readership.

I am fully aware that no author should be prepared to publish, as it stands, a work that is written quite deliberately in a spirit of true candour during the lifetime of the people he discusses. It is not that I write maliciously or with any intention to be unkind. But I do realise that in publishing my autobiography on my internet website, a large quantity of the material will need to be withheld, until such a time as the last person who is featured in the text has expired. I have also thought it advisable to conceal behind the letters of the alphabet the precise names of many participants within this story, for reasons of tact. But I remain hopeful that the completed work will be regarded as a considerable literary accomplishment, which may be taken – alongside the murals – as among the most significant of my life's achievements.

If after a century has elapsed the world at large can detect that progress is being made towards the goals that I have been at pains to discuss over the course of these particular essays and, more generally, within my autobiography as a whole, then I'd be happy in such retrospective understanding. But I do not set much likelihood in there being an afterlife. I am content to settle for an intuitive conviction that these things will eventually come to pass – a visionary's faith that what he imagines is as concrete as the established reality perceived by another man's eye. The notion that I have discerned it creates a good measure of peace of mind in my attitude to life. It is this perhaps which constitutes the character of my niche within the universe.

20

The Purpose of Life

We find ourselves in existence not from any act of choice which we ourselves made but from the choice of parents with whom we may (or may not) build up satisfactory bonds of relationship. In some cases parents may instil us with their own sense of purpose in life: an inspiration to continue with some particular problem-solving quest, to the attainment of specific goals, which may involve a replication of their own achievements or the fulfilment of a prowess which was desired but not realised within their lives. On the other hand we may find ourselves creating our own sense of purpose from ideas which derive entirely from our experience.

No matter which the approach, the notion of a purpose in life stands central to any lasting sense of involvement with this universe in which we all dwell for whatever span of years that we find to be our lot. Provided that we achieve some degree of success in implementing this sense of purpose, it will contribute greatly towards both our self-esteem and our peace of mind; and a society in which self-esteem and peace of mind can be widely promoted amongst the individuals it is comprised of furnishes us with the best possible formula for attainment of the general happiness.

These are conditions we need to watch when assessing our individual ability to align ourselves with the dictates of our universe. The universe may be a gentle master so long as we can find a way of tending to its needs within the realisation of our own personalised identity. It promptly emerges in the guise of an ogre if we establish our own interests on a level too much aside from, or above, those of the common lot.

It also displays random tantrums, which may well destroy the lives (or just the well-being) of individuals deserving a better fate. The random strike of death or misfortune on a tranquil day must be anticipated as part of a pattern into which the history of each and every one of us has been woven. Naturally we hope for better things, but we must be ready to shield ourselves from dismay if disaster should befall.

It is after all best that we should live in acceptance of the idea that our experience is contained within a strictly finite life, upon a planet whose history is finite, within a universe which is itself finite – despite the fact that it seems to stand there in permanence and in perpetuity. There can be little purpose in fretting over what our individual lot may turn out to be, provided that we are currently doing all within our power to fulfil the sense of purpose on this earth to which we have committed ourselves.

We all find ourselves with a number of perceived problems on our plate. We must tackle these in the spirit of a problem-solving quest and awareness that each solution we adopt may unleash problems of a different kind. Our concern should never be to withdraw from this quest, rather to be careful to ensure that the problems on our plate are decreased, not augmented, by the solutions we choose to adopt.

Each individual's quest is a highly personalised affair. There are no general rules on offer. But the creation of one's special niche within society – indeed, within the universe at large – involves a variety of routine practices which most people take for granted. Each individual needs to establish what will be the family form from which he will be making his attack upon fortune. He will need to be clear as to the nature of the political groupings whose ideals may be sufficiently similar to his own to warrant a joint approach in quest for solutions. He must also be clear on the identity of the state which will permit such political groups to operate with the necessary degree of freedom to have some possibility of attaining their goals; and he must know what legitimate assistance and encouragement he can expect to receive from this state.

Regardless of any assistance that the individual might anticipate will come his way, it would be wise for him to realise that throughout his existence he should be capable of standing on his own feet in the pursuit of goals he has freely chosen. It is usual that he would have selected for himself a territorial base, or home nest, from which to operate. The concept of a home is important in that it stands as the point of connection between the individual and the universe. Without it, he is rootless and at a disadvantage. From inside it, he confronts the rest of the world as if from behind a shield.

Though we find ourselves in this world without either requesting or arranging that we should be here, we are liable to accept the fact, because suicide represents too negative and irreversible a solution. The identification of a purpose in life may be largely a survival technique, but it is also a key to human happiness. Beyond finding his own generalised approach to the problems of living, the individual will have much work left to do in discovering where his special talents for involvement might lie. That work is what makes the humanity in us start smouldering, hopefully to ignite as something more inspirational than a damp squib, so that our thoughts and aspirations may finally explode in a brilliance of radiation throughout mankind.

21

The Longleat Experience

It was a piece of magnificent good fortune that I found myself born into the expectation of inheriting Longleat. In fact ever since 1953, when I was 21 and my parents were divorcing, I have been the only adult member of the Thynn family to reside permanently in the house; and ever since 1956 I have been running the Longleat estate, with the exception of the park and its tourist attractions, which my father always kept firmly under his control. After his death on 30th June 1992, however, all aspects of the Longleat organisation were unified; so that nowadays they are finally running in harmony.

The period while I was (so to speak) waiting in the wings was in some ways difficult for me. I had no wish to trespass upon my father's role in fronting the Longleat image with all of his considerable charm and showmanship, so I just got on with my own business, preparing the bulk of my work, both artistic and literary, so that I could turn it over to the service of Longleat once the time did finally arrive.

The murals I have painted, on removable sheets of chipboard covering the walls of my private apartments, stand as the greatest evidence of those years of laborious toil. There are indeed several ways in which these murals might be assessed. Some of them I categorise as 'cocoons' – the idea of me being like a caterpillar who views all his own handiwork looking up and out from the inside, with a feeling perhaps that this constitutes his vision of the universe.

I have painted several such cocoons, giving over the walls of particular rooms to such themes as 'The Ages of Man' or 'The Ages of History' or 'Noah's Ark' or 'A Mural of Formative Footsteps' or 'An Autobiographical Mural' or 'A Mural of Wessex Identity'. Each cocoon furnishes a visual depiction of the way I see myself in relation to some wider concept – various visions of the cradle that contains me, so to speak. They prepare me for identifying with those concepts, or even with the universe at large. Then there is 'Bluebeard's

Collection' where I have put on display the heads of my wifelets within a spiral staircase, or the 'Ancestral Heads' which adorn the other spiral staircase. Here are hung the heads of many an ancestor, whether patrilineal or matrilineal; the bulk of them, however, are in the new banqueting suite up on the top floor. These two collections might likewise be categorised as cocoons, in that they represent my ideas of broader family identification.

I have also painted another category of mural, which might be described as 'therapies'. These relate to the type of painting that is prescribed for institutionalised lunatics, furnishing them with some visual depiction of the anxieties that come welling up inside, to enable them to begin to try to regulate it themselves, or even to modify their expression. Some examples of my therapies are 'The Paranoia Murals', 'Mental Disorder', 'The Quest for Compatibility between the Sexes', 'The Transition from Prey to Predator', 'Heaven and Hell', 'Life and Death', 'Food', 'The Kama Sutra Mural' (where I am ridding myself of sexual inhibitions) and 'The Disco Mural' (where I am urging myself to emerge from introversion towards extroversion). In yet another area, 'The Abstract Conversation Pieces' exercise my organisational skills, which is in itself a therapy, as I prove to myself that I can orchestrate the work of several young art students so that the sequence turns out as a cohesive art display.

Finally there is a category for 'fantasies', which constitute the murals that I painted to decorate the walls of the nursery suite, where my children were brought up. My purpose here was to surround them with a fantasy atmosphere in which children of all races would be displayed in a spirit of co-operation, not only with each other but also with the animal kingdom. I had the walls of four rooms to cover, for which I took the themes of 'Daytime', 'Night-time', 'Underground' and 'Underwater'.

As a result of spending much of a lifetime in the painting of these murals, I have never had the opportunity of showing my work in a picture gallery and thus getting to know what its market price might be. But it would have been absurd for me to forego the unique opportunity I possessed to display whatever I might paint on the walls of the palatial museum where I happened to dwell – in apartments that would eventually have a significant proportion of the West Country's tourists flocking to see them. What artist could have decided differently?

That being said, there does remain some intention in the back of my mind that one day I might paint a retrospective sequence of new murals – an additional 'Age of Man' perhaps, or an additional 'Age of History', plus another 'Disco Panel' and another 'Paranoia Panel', until all phases of my past work have been reconstructed and put up for sale in a belated exhibition of my work elsewhere than at Longleat. That way I should at last discover the prices that I might command for any subsequent commissions of my work.

The environment of Longleat has in fact determined the nature of my life, and even the style in which I paint, since I was from the outset formulating that style to concur with the decor and atmosphere of the rooms where I was painting. This didn't involve any slavish loyalty to precedent art styles. The lovely thing about Longleat is that it has always been and still is evolving. There is as great a justification for displaying there how the Thynn family chose to live in the 20th century as for how they did in Victorian times. And there is still ample scope for subsequent generations of Thynns to leave their appropriate mark up on the top floor, in lavish depiction of decor in the 21st century!

Longleat furnishes the most sumptuous of backdrops against which any family could aspire to enact its lives. I am akin to the individual polyp dedicated to the task of embellishing my particular corner of his coral reef. I relish the opportunities, while revering the traditions and the discipline over me which the situation entails. I hope to have enriched those traditions before passing them down to future generations of Thynns.

22

Peace of Mind and Prayer

If we are fortunate, we shall have created for ourselves a personal niche within society which involves the ability, and the opportunity, to fix our attention and our endeavours upon those problems whose solution we can envisage; and we shall be doing this from the base camp of a territory that we regard as our personal home, with the intimate support of the family that we have chosen for ourselves, if not with the more general backing of political groups consisting of like-minded individuals intent upon the same goals. If all of this is running smoothly, the reward that we may anticipate for ourselves is peace of mind.

The individual who attains peace of mind is at one with the universe. It encompasses him or her in its bosom, in the serenity of its eternal permanence. This is a condition of being which may be attained not only by persistent application towards the realisation of work goals, but also by the performance of physico-spiritual exercises such as yoga or meditation. Proficiency in these might accentuate the individual's capacity for adopting a frame of mind where his interests fuse more harmoniously with those of the universe in its totality. He may start to think, and to motivate himself, from this unit which is so immensely more vast than himself. The concepts of self and the ego may by such a process be merged into something akin to deistic will.

A big question remains as to whether there can be direct communication between the individual and this concept of deity, which of course can be identified as none other than the universe as a whole; there is also the reciprocal question of whether the universe as a whole can communicate its will (or its best interests) to the individuals who comprise society at large. Much of course will depend upon the sensitivity of the individual to the dictates of the universe; and the techniques previously mentioned for attainment of serenity in life may well prove an invaluable training for these purposes. I think it

entirely possible that particular individuals, through a cerebral statement of what they desire to see enacted in life, may in fact influence
the outcome of events.

Populations are prone to psychosomatic influences, so the perceived will of any portion of the human race may well on occasion get
translated into a generally desired change. Something similar may be
the case with individuals who wish to influence the actions of other
individuals. An awareness may gradually augment the extent to
which others may wish us to switch in our volition, with the result
that our behaviour eventually becomes directed towards different
(and otherwise surprising) ends. Such influence from the persuasive
quality of thought, which is in fact central to the whole concept of
prayer, is never stronger than when the values represented in such
thought lie closest to the hub of cohesion for the human race – or for
the cohesion of the human race with the totality of the universe.

The distinction between man's twin religious concerns, either to
influence his fellow men towards some concept of improved behaviour or to ensure (no matter what happens) that he himself will attain
peace of mind, highlights the difference between active and passive
temperaments when confronted with the problems of life. Prayer
might be seen as an endeavour to find solutions for those problems,
whereas the quest for the serenity in peace of mind is more a question
of attaining an appropriate mental attitude despite the existence of
the problems. But the two concepts do relate to one another in that
the man who wishes to discover the efficacy of prayer might be best
advised to seek it in conjunction with the attainment of peace of
mind. And the man who has attained serenity in this fashion is that
much more liable to influence his fellow men towards actions which
he deems both good and right.

The cultural pattern for the human population within different
parts of this planet gets divided quite largely for the reason displayed
here. There are parts of the world where the potential for individual
persuasion might be rated higher than elsewhere. Democratic
regimes (as we understand them) may encourage individuals to
assert an active influence over political change. It should therefore
come as no surprise that the efficacy of prayer has been advocated
and developed in those same parts of the globe, whereas in the East
(where populations have traditionally often been obliged to watch the
struggle for political power strictly from the sidelines) the value of a

separate pursuit of peace of mind has taken religious precedence. But the world of the future might well bear witness to a fusion of these impulses.

The ideal for the pantheist, perhaps, should be to investigate his bonding with the universe until he reaches a point where the serenity of peace of mind comes to him as a natural fulfilment of his life's pursuit of a particular problem-solving quest. His thoughts and objectives in the public arena may then become translucently apparent, to the degree that other humans become aware of his personality. Whether or not he might then choose to formulate his hopes for the world (or just for particular individuals) in terms of prayer becomes immaterial. The fact that such an individual actually wishes for these things to come to pass might well be sufficient to trigger their enaction, for he will be recognised by then as a catalyst in his own right.

23

Utopia, or Optimism for a New World Order

There are always some amongst us who manage to conceive in the mind's eye the vision of some greatly improved world order, which is promptly accredited with the improbable perfection of Utopia. We are instantly presented with a path for its attainment which is fraught with pitfalls. As a start, anyone who attempts to play the visionary's game in perceiving such a pattern for the future evolution of the socio-political order on this planet in terms that are even remotely idealistic renders himself vulnerable to the charge that his vision is divorced from reality. We never have far to look before we discern the most terrible departures from (or reversals of) the ideal, to an extent that our doubts may increase concerning its practicability. But if one such vision is found to be faulty, then we still are required to fix our eyes upon another; for a world without vision amounts to a world without hope.

Idealism of one kind or another is necessary for mankind as a directional rudder – as an aid to the translation of values into action on the spur of spontaneous thought. But such thought only comes readily to mind once a vision has been worked out and fully comprehended. Having reached that point, we may be wise to suspend further analysis and embrace our vision as a matter of faith, putting our efforts to its service in the hopes of furthering its evolution towards the goals already foreseen.

Before taking that leap of faith, it is only right that we should have examined the alternatives. In contrast to my personal vision of a democratic regionalist future for the world, where individual mothers will select the family form most appropriate for themselves within a polymorphous society, in accordance with their particular religious principles beneath a broad umbrella of a pantheistic world faith, others may approach the visionary game with predictions of an altogether different kind. This conflict of opinion may become a means of identifying the problems which might emerge in the opposing vision's case and thus contribute to reducing the probability that mankind will in fact move in such a direction. We will be deterred from doing so by an increasing recognition of the unhappiness or suffering that such change might entail, with this being assessed against such unhappiness and suffering as are involved in permitting society to remain static and unchanged. When the benefit from caution and restraint is found wanting, then evolution of some description eventually becomes inevitable and unstoppable. But of course the true value of any visionary's predictions can only be assessed in hindsight.

From those who express horror and despair concerning what is going on in our world, we should always demand some alternative vision of directions in which progress might be made. The terrifying examples of both Communism and Fascism in practice over recent history were sufficient to deflect my own vision from any totalitarian solution to world problems. Religious fundamentalism of whatever kind evokes similar nightmare vistas of fanatical intolerance. For my personal vision, I need to explore all avenues where a tolerant and democratic liberalism prevails, no matter how dire the circumstances which may arise within its socio-political framework. I would tend to argue that the problems which arise are almost always attributable to factions which seek to implement authoritarian ideas, intolerantly; this in theory at least might involve us in the adoption of a similar ruthlessness to combat them, but only to the point when their disestablishment has been obtained. The quest for evolution of true democracy then returns as the necessary persuasion.

We are obliged to anticipate that the path of progress will never be entirely smooth. There will indeed be times which give rise to discouragement or even despair. But there is compensation in the thought that there have seldom been huge bounds of human advancement without us first encountering huge depths of misery, in which the nature of the problem field could be perceived for what it really was. It is only from a mutually empathetic understanding of essential problems, with people's antagonism towards proposed solutions expressed with unmitigated candour, that the most practicable solutions (or compromises) are liable to get stated, and finally to emerge as new realities.

We may perceive the world's suffering for what it truly is but at the same time envisage solutions along paths which we hope may arrive at the establishment of the new world order. We need the vision of that ideal to inspire us through the whole task of living. It doesn't represent any certainty for our lives, because there is no such certainty ever to be found. But it does furnish us with the desire to continue our participation in life, even with confidence that we are on the right side, and to persevere in doing the right things.

Another way of phrasing it would be to say that we discover how we have allied ourselves with the best interests of the totality of the universe, to a point where all the long term forces at work within this universe must inevitably be on our side. That represents a feeling that any devout pantheist should be seeking to attain; and with it may come an optimism that all must work out in the way we envision it in the end. Short term reversals can then be taken in stride, in the confidence that our goals will ultimately be attained.

There is thus a new world order that lies almost within our grasp. Emergent generations are perhaps those who will acknowledge its arrival. This will coincide with the attainment of World Government, as predicted in my essay on that subject[1]; an era which will be initiated by an act of political agreement by the majority of mankind, rather than by the birth-date of any prophet or holy man. It will be an era when the populations of this planet finally come together to initiate a new society, for a new world. The old order will become a thing of the past, for this will truly be a new beginning and the opportunity at last to create the long-awaited Utopia.

---

[1] Essay 11. See also Essay 14.

24

Playing God

We find ourselves at the summit of life's biological tree of creatures on this planet, in a pre-eminence of power which the dinosaurs before us knew for far longer than has been our present lot. From our study of their fate we know how such colossi of life's destiny can quite suddenly be rendered vulnerable after some unforeseen event like the catastrophic impact of a huge meteor. All manner of life stands permanently at risk from the vagaries of a yet insufficiently predictable universe. So there is no certainty that we shall remain supreme here on earth, although we are entitled to assume this supremacy until such a time as we encounter superior beings – from an extraterrestrial civilisation, or wherever.

In the realisation that the laurels of our supreme position may be handed to others far sooner than we might anticipate, or even that events within the universe may extinguish our own species as it has done to others before, our role in the meantime should be to endeavour to merit the advantageous position we have inherited as a result of all the self-improvement in our human ancestors. Rather than exploit this position, we are liable to endure for considerably longer if we can find our way to deserve the top dog position by committing ourselves, and our influence, to the benefit of living creatures as a whole. Our approach to the subject of self-interest should then expand to incorporate the interests of life in its entirety.

In thus 'playing God', we'll automatically evolve into being far more worthy creatures than we are at present. The adoption of vegetarian diet will be but a small instance of our reformed habits, although it might well prove possible for us to contrive that what we eat is no less tasty and textured than our contemporary fare. But it will be in the way that we learn to foster the green ecology of our planet's various environmental settings that will perhaps establish how well we are fitted to fulfil this role – to the benefit of all.

As individual human beings, our personal morality will need to reflect our constant concern for the well-being of all creatures, with a full understanding of the diverse cultures of our planet's human populations, in the full knowledge of their histories and their sociological aspirations. There will be no limit to the quantity that we can discover about our human development and the origins of our civilisation in the archaeological remains of previous such endeavours. We need to perceive how the entire world has developed, in communion and interreaction with all that can be encountered within this universe, and how these lines of communication can be kept open and preserved.

Our personalities under the influence of this evolution will gradually change, as we learn to identify at ever deeper levels with the concerns of others. We'll learn to speak and think with the interests of the world at heart. Prayer will take the form of articulating communal interest, until it becomes what indeed we think, while thoughts which conflict with such intent will promptly be recognised as the embodiment of evil.

We must not shy away from this role that we are embracing. Playing God, whether we like it or not, is now our destiny. But of course, we do not wish to be guilty of hubris. So it might be preferable to state that we regard ourselves as the self-appointed agents for all that is good within the universe; and we live our lives in eager anticipation of aligning our efforts with whomever else shall emerge in that universe with a similar calling. We do so in the knowledge that we shall inevitably discover ourselves to be on the same side, as allies in the promotion of the universe's best interests. We are thus all of us like soldiers in the service of God.

We perceive the universe and revere the universe, whether in its fiercest wrath or in its gentlest benevolence. It exists timeless, and we are inevitably a part of its permanence. Under our encouragement and tutelage, the fauna and flora of our planet will attain their best opportunity to thrive. But sensitive discernment will still be required in judging which of them needs to be contained, or even removed, so that the welfare of the majority can be maintained.

We have in our hands the capacity to tailor the attitude to life of forthcoming generations of our descendants. The persuasion should be with us to ensure that their values are nurtured towards these ends. Concern for our planet and for the life which it contains should emerge as paramount in all their thinking hours, involving as it does a systematic re-education of their hearts.

Such is the stature of our aims, and the criterion by which we must be ready to judge ourselves, as to the worthiness of our acceptance of this mantle which we have taken up to wear. We shall be carrying with us these responsibilities for as long as our lives endure, with the additional expectation for us to ensure that there will be others to take over the same functions before we die. Then, in the knowledge that all has been done which could be done, we shall finally be ready to retire from life with a fully deserved peace of mind – until the next repetition of the time-cycle, wherein we shall be back again to re-enact precisely the same role, and with precisely the same degree of success or failure.

25

Pantheistic Texts

Within this series of twenty-five essays, of which this is the last, I have been at pains to indicate the structure around which my attitudes took shape. The moral and political aspects have all been indicated. But if an attitude is to acquire the significance of a religion, its precepts should be clearly stated within the form of a creed. For a pantheist this might be as follows:

> I BELIEVE in the singleness of this one and only universe, in all its comprehensive totality, existing in permanence and in perpetuity, and within which I occupy (as part of it) my own selected niche of an individual character. Within the permanence of this universe, I believe in the perpetuity of my own life history, so that both birth and death are mere incidental points along its track. I believe that the process of living brings out qualities which suggest values, which then create personal goals that inspire me with a sense of purpose in life, during the fulfilment of which I may hope to attain both self-esteem and peace of mind. I believe that my status as a human being, regardless of my character or abilities, entitles me to certain rights which others of my species should respect. But I also believe in the natural dignity of all living species, and their own right to respect for its preservation. I believe in the glorious mystery of all living creatures, and of the environment which contains them, along with my capacity to be of service to their interests.

The nature of our most fervent aspirations might be expressed in the form of a prayer, where the individual addresses himself to his particular concept of the deity:

> WE STAND in our isolation, both desiring and seeking to achieve our alignment with the consensus persuasion of all the influences currently operating within this wondrous universe. We acknowledge its perma-

nence in perpetuity, and we revere its totality to the point of worship. We shall endeavour to discern its demands upon our lives, and upon our environment, and commit our personal labour towards the attainment of those ends.

May we cultivate a heartfelt respect and gratitude for the labour of others, who have furnished us with the wherewithal to enjoy the benefits of life: the farmers and foresters who have cultivated our crops, the manufacturers and retailers who have clothed us or otherwise kept us supplied, the teachers who have instructed us, the doctors and healers who have kept us in good health, the scientists, artists and entertainers who have enriched the quality of living, the legislators and adjudicators who have established the rules that facilitate the conduct of a civilised society and the enforcers of these rules in our protection from those who might endanger us. And may they always offer their services to us, in appreciation of the true long term requirements of this universe.

Let us live this day in a spirit finely attuned to the needs of all other living beings, so that our actions may reflect their best interests as much as our own. And in the absence of others better fitted than ourselves to assume the protective role that all living creatures both require and deserve, let us rise to the challenge in performing that role ourselves, to the best of our abilities and without concern for personal benefit or reward.

In our faith that the universe contains all things wonderful, as well as all things terrible, may we strive to influence the outcome of events so that the greatest happiness of the greatest number is effectively promoted at all levels where the concept of happiness is comprehensible; and within the communion of spirit which this commitment implies, may we find the means to band together with those of a like spirit, in the realisation of these ideals over the widest possible spread of the universe at large.

Perhaps the most frequent requirement for a religious statement occurs when we are asked to say the grace before a meal. A text that we knew in childhood might then be adapted thus:

MAY WHAT is before us be received with pleasure, in appreciation of the effort that others spent in its production, and of the earth's fruitfulness in yielding it to their hands.

Central to any religion, we might expect to find the existence of some holy book, like the *New Testament* or the *Koran*. In the case of pantheism, the ultimate version of such a text has yet to be written; but we may expect it to furnish us with a complete cosmology – a scientifically authentic account of the past history of this universe, and the anticipated course of its future history until the time of its gravitational projection into the monoblock. It is in our reverence for the totality of this universe, for the manner in which it exercises its own form of stability within the permanence of the time cycle, and for the manner in which our particular brand of individualism is enabled to flourish within it, that the concept of pantheism as a religion takes root. But we should never lose sight of the fact that it only serves us as an umbrella religion, with the finer detail for worship dictated from within the religious tradition through which we arrived within its comprehensive embrace.

My delineation of pantheism, and all that it entails, is now perhaps as clear as I can make it. Its practice, however, is quite another matter, and something that I shall be trying to acquire over the years that remain to me.

Appendix:

Speeches in the House of Lords

1: Universal Nursery Education, 19th January 1994

MY LORDS, I would like to voice my support for the idea of universal nursery education. But I remain concerned over the choice in the direction which this could take, according to whether or not it should be introduced as an integral part of the state system.

My preference for the concept of state education, even at its nursery level, relates to the value I attach to a fully integrated society. Although I myself am an unashamed product of the private system in education – I enjoyed it greatly, and might even claim to have been successful whilst there – I chose the comprehensive system for my children because of it being less class-divisive. If we promote a system where the majority of those who are affluent send their children to private schools, whilst those who are devoid of affluence send theirs through the state system, then we entrench the class divisions in society in a manner where they are likely to endure over the course of that entire generation.

Universal nursery education offers each community the possibility of a bonding experience, even if their subsequent educational tracks should differ. I believe in the importance of such bonding. I'd be happier of course if the Government were to advocate a more prolonged period of shared educational experience, in that the bonding would then be even greater – with its consequent diminishment in the class divisiveness such as we know it today. But I'd like to think that whatever the Government now proposes might be regarded as an initial step towards such an eventual universal-ization of the whole schooling process.

The bonding experience is perhaps more important still to those who are disadvantaged within our society, and I am particularly concerned for the welfare of one such group – namely single parents: both single mothers or single fathers, incidentally – where the existence of nursery education will be invaluable. The position of single parents is currently under threat:

especially in the case of unmarried mothers. It might be anything from the proposed loss of benefits, to the question of reverse discrimination in their application for housing. There is also a suggestion that the Government might be intending to force them into the monogamous fold with threats of disadvantage while they choose to remain single.

One of the threats is that benefits could only be paid to them via the grandparents – even when this might be seen as the denial of an adult's option to set up house on her own. Or there is talk about obliging single parents (as a condition that has to be met before benefits are on offer) to dwell together in distinctly unlisted buildings, which might otherwise be ready for demolition – a suggestion that could be paraphrased as driving them into ghettos. On raising such a family within the disadvantaged environment which our society creates for them, they find their children categorized as potentially criminal. This may take the form of a statistical forecast, which is then offered as spurious justification for pressing the case for adoption, which goes against any mother's natural inclination to raise a child herself.

It is a matter of great importance to single parents that free nursery education should be on offer and readily available at the hands of the state. With all the problems peculiar to her situation, the knowledge that her children are in safe professional hands throughout the time of day renders such a parent the freedom to get back to work. Even prior to nursery schooling, there should be day-care centres and play schools, which would furnish her children with the most appropriate arena for that initial bonding with the rest of society. When objection is raised about the expense to the taxpayer on this issue, then the cost should be measured against the reward to all of us in the attainment of an integrated society, and in the satisfactory development even of its more disadvantaged members.

I would like to stress that single parents frequently do not choose this status for themselves – it often takes the form of an unintended situation, which arises to clobber them (so to speak) from out of the blue. When it does arise as something planned, then it should not be our role as legislators to punish them because they did not choose differently. A mother's freedom of choice as to the family form that might suit her the best should be respected no matter what form this takes. It is the psychological welfare of her children, even if we have personal reservations on the advisability of her choice, which should emerge as our prime concern. So it is especially (but not solely) in the interests of single parent families that I beg you, my lords, to do all that is possible to accelerate the introduction of both day-care centres and nursery education in general.

2: Devolution: Wessex Home Rule, 19th May 1997

WHILE I am delighted by the Government's intention to introduce a measure of self-government for both Scotland and Wales, I am concerned that there are no plans to follow this with a reappraisal of the constitutional status of the English regions – unless there should be some demand in evidence that this might be desired. So I feel bound to proclaim that interest for the inhabitants of Wessex. And I am hopeful that there will be similar demands from all of the other regions. For I would like to think that the UK might now be approaching the time when devolution will be introduced on an even wider scale, and that the intended legislation on behalf of Scotland and Wales will set a pattern for what might be applied elsewhere.

The appeal of devolution is that it offers a region far greater control over its own quality of life, while encouraging cultural diversity between different regions in a manner that will individualistically enhance the lives of those who dwell there: without interfering in the concept of a broader based UK sovereignty, under whose aegis the macro-economics and the defence of the realm will continue to be organised on their behalf. Such emphasis upon regional individualism would be felt as a balancing counterpart to the ever-increasing centralisation in the way our lives get run.

At this point in time when we stand on the brink of fuller co-operation with Europe, it would be a move greatly appreciated by the other nations, whose regional structure is already significantly stronger than our own, if this country should present itself in terms of a more pronounced geographical definition of the English regions, furnishing them with new political responsibility to enhance their emergent identities. That way, it will prove easier for us to emerge in a constitutional shape that will enable us to guide, rather than to hinder, the formation of a European political union yet to come: in the forefront, rather than following in the wake, of a movement which I anticipate will be shaping our identity over the coming half century.

It can certainly be argued that the English regions don't even know where their boundaries should be drawn. But the heartlands are where these identities have been best preserved; and I would like to think that these could be made the distinct nuclei around which the concept of their re-emergence might be encouraged. Prior to the proposal of any specific legislation on behalf of the English regions, however, I am hoping that the

Government will initiate a consideration of these matters within the county councils which are responsible for the welfare of these heartlands.

In the case of Wessex, I believe that the government should invite the county councils of the five counties which constitute Central Wessex – the councils of Dorset, Somerset, Wiltshire, Berkshire and Hampshire – to meet together to discuss and determine the areas where their quality of life might be collectively improved, with a view to realising a greater sense of cultural fusion and economic welfare. (Each of these counties might be expected to host such assemblies on a rota basis.) I hasten to add that this would not constitute an additional tier of government. It would be the councillors already elected within these counties who would have the right to attend these assemblies. And it would be only be at a later date, if this government chose to set up a Wessex Witan on an official basis, that there would be a requirement for councillors to be elected to it direct – replacing the existing county council elections.

Once the Wessex Witan was already functional, at a later date – I might suggest some five years later – the areas which surround Central Wessex would need to determine whether or not they might wish to proclaim themselves as lying within the borders of Wessex, or within the borders of a neighbouring region, whose heartland I am anticipating will have acquired similar political identity at the same time as ourselves. I am foreseeing that a future map of England will include the following list of regions: Wessex, South Thames, North Thames, Trent and Anglia, Middle England, Lancastria, Yorkshire, Northumbria – a total of eight regions in all. And the process of determining whether some particular segment of a county belongs here, or there, should only be made after establishing the preferences in a series of local referenda.

The case for determining the precise borders of Wessex is as delicate as with many another region. There are areas, like the Isle of Wight, West Sussex, Buckinghamshire, Oxfordshire, Gloucestershire, Devon and Cornwall, where I would certainly wish to be guided by local feeling before proclaiming that they were to be included within the Wessex identity. Being half Cornish myself, I know that Cornwall proudly proclaims its separate identity – even from Devon. But if the region were to be presented as 'Wessex and Cornwall', with special emphasis upon the Cornish people being firmly in control of their own quality of life, then I cannot predict where they might finally elect to stand – as a separate region, or in association with Wales and Brittany, or in association with an extended Wessex. But these I regard as problems which lie beyond the establishment of a

Speeches

political heartland for Wessex.

A problem which perhaps worries us the most of all concerns whether the creation of these regions might incur additional taxation, to be levied in surplus to that which is under the strict control of our central government. For the regional assemblies will indeed require funds to finance their useful activities. I am wondering if a system might not be possible where each of these assemblies would receive a per capita and per hectare rebate from the Inland Revenue that has been collected throughout the United Kingdom as a whole. And this sum would be theirs to spend as they might wish, in lieu of funds that would formerly have been at each county council's disposal.

The concept of an England regionalised will stand in total contrast to what we were beginning to become – an England which had lost its empire, while failing to identify a role in the world which it now could play. The creation of a separate parliament for Scotland, and an assembly for Wales, will certainly be steps in the right direction. But I sincerely hope that this government will not miss out on such a unique opportunity to make catalytic decisions that will ultimately bring both Britain and Europe into the 21st century.

3: The Importance of the Arts in the Life of the Nation, 18th March 1998

MY LORDS, a nation gets awarded the character that it deserves. By neglecting to promote some aspect of this character, that aspect becomes increasingly insignificant within the image which other nations regard as our worth. And this might also hold true for the way future generations of our own nation come to regard what we ourselves were worth.

The evidence is abundant that here in Britain we have the potential to excel in the performance of all the arts. But these arts can only truly flourish when given patronage and financial encouragement. The potential is certainly there, but it is for society to bring it to fruition; and it is for government to give society the necessary lead on how this can be done.

There is a danger if the arena for artistic performance is permitted to become too centralised, with the regions required to focus upon what is going on within the capital city to discover the potential of their own individualistic excellence. The situation will become healthier if we can revive the notion of there being a thriving local culture within each region, proud of its own traditions, and of its aesthetic potential.

Government should therefore assume the responsibility to promote the re-emergence of the English regions, so that they are encouraged to create their own local artistic excellence in distinction from one another, and in competition with one another to draw the maximum number of tourists to come and be entertained in the significant regional manner. But this should involve the creation of regional assemblies, whose main purpose will be to tailor the quality of life within that territory, so that its true individualism can be perceived for what it best might become.

It should also be the responsibility of the regional assemblies to promote the full artistic potential of those who are still at school through the format of the education that they put on offer. There should be state-run schools within each of the regional systems, specialising in some particular aspect of the arts – whether that might be specifically in the arts, in music, or in drama. And it could be said in passing that this might be paralleled in schools for sporting excellence too.

Then once our artists have left the nest, so to speak, Government should promote the keenness of regional competition through the constant incentive of prizes – not exclusively for artists who dwell in those regions, but on an international basis, so that artists from other cultures feel encouraged to come to these shores to compete with our native talent and, in so doing, introduce elements of their cultures to inspire the participants within our own.

Then finally there is the question of improved display: a display at sites of easy access for the region as a whole. It should not be necessary for an aspirant artist to visit the capital city to discover the inspiration for his native art. The finest collections should be on his very doorstep. And the regional assemblies should be in a position to allot funds to transform existing museums so that they can fulfil this required function – funds which should also be used to put on arts festivals where the special chararacter of the region can be publically proclaimed.

The artistic potential of the nation is thus indirectly linked to the Government's ability to enable the English regions to re-emerge in a spirit of their most colourful individualism. So the most significant step which government could take today, in the encouragement of the arts, will be in the creation of our regional assemblies; and I urge that this step should be taken without delay.

4: Hereditary Peers, 25th October 1998

MY LORDS, while regarding with pride the role that our hereditary peers have played, historically, within the government of this country, I do regard it as important at this final juncture that we who hitherto have held a role in government from right of birth should be seen to accept that this should change – which implies that a majority of us should go down on record as supporting the Government in its intention to remove our voting powers. There is no social justice within a situation where we might expect to retain such privilege, and I trust that we shall be seen to assist in this constitutional change.

Before we depart, however, there is still the opportunity for us to let our feelings be known on the nature your lordships' house should take once we have gone – my hope being that it will become something even more different to that other place, so that new aspects of the national identity might come to the fore within the continuing debate on the form which our governmental institutions should take.

If in another place party politics should continue to thrive in representation by constituency, I am hopeful that in your lordships' house there might be special emphasis upon our regional identity, and upon our European identity. We should regard this as the opportunity to introduce these new alignments within our national identity, in order that we should be readying ourselves for a political future much in contrast to what exists today.

There are different means by which these new alignments could probably be emphasised so that this house becomes no mere reflection of that other place. I envisage that this house might broadly consist of two distinct categories of life peer. The first might be nominated by a special committee appointed by the party leaders, not so much because of their party service but because of their national pre-eminence within one field or another. These peers would furnish the essential background of professional knowledge, which would continue to characterise the debates within your lordships' house.

The second element should be concerned to emphasise the regional and European perspectives, with a list of life peers put forward by each of the eight English regions, as well as a list from Scotland, one from Wales and one from Northern Ireland, selected by the county councils within each of the regions (or nations) concerned. And it would be the task of these same peers to investigate the full potential of co-operation between our own regions and those of Europe, and then to promote this concept of a United Regions of Europe even prior to its actual inception.

If the concept of a Council of the Isles is to be developed further, with its particular concern for any Irish problems that might remain, then I envisage that your lordships' house, thus evolved, and sitting in concert no doubt with an Irish delegation, could become the arena where they might the most judiciously be resolved.

A reformation of your lordships' house on these lines would place it at the forefront of constitutional reform as we move into the next century. Our task would no longer be a mere source of review for legislation that has been decided in another place. What I am suggesting would establish your lordships' house as the centrepiece for our national transformation towards an emergent identity, which I anticipate will be based upon Europe and its regions.

Far from suggesting that this house will stand in rivalry, opposition or antagonism to another place, I envisage that it will be opening up a whole new area for our identity in full fellowship with all that went before, and with all who remain in control of these matters.

I welcome the fact that our Government should now be clearing the decks, so that those who determine the precise form that your lordships' new house will attain should not include those who have taken our seats on a hereditary basis. But I sincerely hope that the Government will not cease its reforming zeal on this measure alone and look forward to the day when this house will furnish the inspirational blueprint for the upper chambers of all other such European assemblies. And I wish those who take their seats in the new house all the influence and success that they deserve.

5: Regional Development Agencies, 25th November 1998

MY LORDS, I express my delight that the Government, by turning its attention to the formation of development agencies for the English regions, is about to create an identity for the English regions which will gradually bring them into direct comparison with the territories of Scotland and Wales. I regard this as a real start towards the conception of a 'United Regions of Britain', which we might regard as a precursor to an eventual 'United Regions of Europe', if not for the world as a whole.

I hope that the Government will be careful at this juncture to get the size of these regions appropriate to the broader purpose of defining the map of

Britain, so that it may serve as an inspiration to the rest of Europe concerning the workings of a truly democratic spirit within the Continent as a whole, for we should envisage that the ideal of one man, one vote, will follow along this path of political evolution to become one region, one vote – for which reason I must stress the importance of getting the boundaries of each region drawn from the very start so that territories of equal gravity are conceived. I am here speaking of an approximation of that equal size in terms of each regional population.

This is really a plea that the Government does not introduce an idea of regions which are too small for such purposes. To speak in terms of a single example, there is a danger that the concept of Wessex could be broken down into a series of smaller regions which certainly have an identity of their own, but which would be too small to furnish the gravity for any future political development of a 'United Regions of Europe'. Despite the fact that western Wessex does not identify closely with eastern Wessex – let alone with northern Wessex – I am concerned that the boundaries of each of the regions should be drawn wider than one might initially conceive of them.

This is not to say that any portion of a region should be coerced into union with another portion. There are bound to be areas which look in two or more different directions concerning where their future cultural identity should lie. Far from advocating that any decisions in such matters should be taken behind their backs, I would ask that such matters be decided by holding local referenda, with local debate on the subject initiated as quickly as possible.

It is most important that the principle of consent should prevail in the creation of these regions. It would be on a point of principle that Cornwall should never be told that it has to join with Wessex, unless Cornishmen proclaim that this is their wish. I think I can say that it would not be, unless the region as a whole were to be called 'Wessex and Cornwall'. I speak here as someone who is half Cornish. I envisage that there may be much 11th hour negotiation between neighbouring counties to determine where the boundaries are to be drawn between any of our English regions.

In order that the Government should not end up with a proliferation of regions that are too small to have appropriate significance for these purposes, I might suggest that they should start with a clear idea of where the regional heartlands might be situated, then add to or subtract from these in accordance with the response from the territories concerned. I am hopeful that by this process the number of regions thus emerging on the new map of England might be just eight. I mentioned those regions in the debate on the gracious Speech at the start of the previous Session so I shall refrain from repeating myself today.

I am urging the Government to give the new development agencies as much gravity as they deem possible, both in terms of their geographical size and in terms of the functions that they might perform. There could be encouragement, for example, that they liaise not only with the development agencies for the other English regions but also with their counterparts in Europe so that the regional approach to government might more easily come into focus.

One of the most important of all the functions for these agencies to perform might be in overseeing the touristic image of their region, inspiring the tourist boards that already exist to present their territory as somewhere most attractive to visit, while coordinating such activities to maximize the effect so that tourists find it easy to perceive the overall character of the region. Perhaps the boards should be amalgamated within any one region so that a conscious effort can be made for them to be promoting the same unified concept, with all the emotional appeal that this involves, thus engendering a desire in the hearts of their tourists to return there frequently. For it is through tourism that all regions will discover their identity – because of their efforts to promote it in competition with all other regions for reasons of pride as well as for financial gain.

I am hopeful that once the development agencies have been established here in England, the Government will consider incorporating the delegates that are appointed by them and by the county councils of their region as life peers within your lordships' house, perhaps to constitute 50 per cent of the total of life peers, for that would truly transform the whole nature of government in this country, and perhaps in Europe too, on regional lines, with the ultimate goal of a 'United Regions of Europe' emerging not far down that road.

6: The Leisure Industries, 13th January 1999

MY LORDS, I should declare a personal interest. In running a stately home, my business lies within these leisure industries which we are now discussing: tourism in particular.

Rurally based leisure industries are emerging very much as the occupational inspiration of our day, which finally reverses a trend which became established at the start of our industrial revolution. Their optimum organisation acquires an increasing importance within the economic welfare of our society. Indeed the significance of tourism has risen so high that it now ranks amongst the foremost of our national industries as an earner of hard currency.

This is a trend which the whole of society can welcome. The over-dependence of any region upon its big cities was always undesirable, in that it encouraged population shifts which left the countryside depleted and sometimes impoverished. So the present switch of emphasis upon the usefulness of activities which can be based at home, and even in the heart of our rural countryside, transforms the very character of the regions in a manner that should be encouraged.

Individually, these leisure industries are small, and they are vulnerable in what for them is a difficult economic climate. Tourism relies to a large extent upon the natural beauty of the local countryside, but also upon the historical and architectural interest that is aroused by the listed buildings that the region contains. Because of their age however, most of these buildings require constant attention and repair to conserve them for what they are.

One of our biggest headaches in this task is the additional cost of the VAT incurred when the work is to be classified as 'repair'. There is VAT to pay for example, if there is an outbreak of death-watch beetle in the roof. It would help us considerably if there were to be zero rating for any such repair work, bringing it into line with those alterations which are categorised as new building work.

My other plea is that simplicity should prevail in the introduction of any new directives concerning such matters as employment, health or safety, much of which emanates from Brussels. We have found it difficult to be economically efficient while the administrative burden is so heavy. Much inconvenience is involved in conforming with all the directives and regulations handed down to us, which needlessly distract us from the task of obtaining optimum performance in these relatively new industries. So simplicity in the legislation (especially from Europe) in establishing the standards to which we must conform will always be appreciated, and found beneficial to these enterprises.

But in more important ways the need to focus upon the European influence is becoming ever more apparent. We in Wessex are well aware of this where tourism is concerned, in the approaches that are being made to us from regions outside Britain, the most significant of which has recently come from the 'Pays de la Loire'. They seek partnership with other tourist regions in Europe as far afield as Germany and Italy to discover the best means for mutual benefit. But they are now seeking partnerships on this side of the Channel too. I believe it was Somerset they approached at the start, but they were looking for something broader based than any single county – until they came to appreciate that the concept of Wessex embraces Somerset and various other counties, so that here was a unit with which the 'Pays de la Loire' could more properly do business.

The Government should encourage this tendency for the leisure industries of one region to commune and communicate with others throughout Europe, to promote the mutual interest by augmenting the flow of tourists around the continent as a whole. Tourism works best if it becomes a general habit, where we go to visit European regions as much as tourists from those regions come to visit ours. The Government should be setting up a framework wherein the regions of Britain can emerge with their own tourist identities, to communicate directly with other regions on that basis.

It is essential that the leisure industries of each region should start to be promoted from a unified regional tourist board, whose purpose is to project the full creative individualism of the region as a whole, so as to attract the maximum number of tourists into their fold. But for this purpose the boundaries between the existing tourist boards do need to be redrawn, so that larger territories are encompassed than what are envisaged today. I believe that the Government should be marking out these tourist regions, with a view to identifying where the borders of the political regions will subsequently be drawn. The creation of these amalgamated tourist boards will set the ball rolling in this most significant direction and is a step that should be taken without delay.

Once these tourist boards have been given the clout that I am anticipating for them, they will apply direct for the European funding of what is becoming an increasingly widespread European concern. The leisure industries are perhaps in the best position to front this trend, to the benefit (while not at the cost) of our national exchequer. And by their co-operation with such Euro-regions, they will be assisting to set up the pattern of a Europe of Regions that will see us into the next century, whereas to omit to do so would involve us getting left behind, and then subsequently out of touch with the way in which our European culture is working out in practice.

7: House of Lords Reform, 22nd February 1999

MY LORDS, I congratulate the Government on producing a White Paper which answers nearly all our questions with regard to a reformed second chamber and which lays down encouraging guidelines on the prospects for further modernisation. It is on this latter subject, however, that I wish to speak.

I take the line that the nation will be best served by a second chamber which stands in complete contrast to the first chamber. I envisage that its members will be appointed in part by an all-party committee, to select peers with the broadest possible expertise and the widest range of professional qualifications. I would like to see them sitting for a ten year period of office, with the committee holding the option to renew their peerages for an additional term, or for half a term, according to what the committee might think best; but with an upper age limit of 75 as the threshold for automatic retirement.

While these might account for half of the peers in the second chamber, I remain anxious that the additional half of your lordships' house will accurately reflect the regional diversity in this land. I feel encouraged that the Government has set up Regional Development Agencies, which will probably emerge as the initial nuclei for the future English regions, although the creation of regional assemblies will also be essential before they can possibly feel that each is emerging into control of its particular quality of life.

I sincerely hope that the Government will encourage these Regions to appear, each within a territory soon to be defined, and of sufficient geographical size to warrant this sense of emergent identity. If they were too small, the purpose would not be served. The smallest region should perhaps be the size of Yorkshire, but in most cases a whole group of counties would be involved, until England might finally consist of eight regions of a similar size in terms of their population. This will furnish the map of England which I envisage will find its place at the heart of European political evolution towards a United Regions of Europe.

But these regions do require cosseting and governmental care in their emergence upon our political scene. And they must surely be given representation within the proposed second chamber, with each of them sending up a delegation of peers, who should be selected by a method parallel to that used for the selection of the other peers, although not by the same all-party committee for the appointment of peers on a national basis. In order to reinforce the idea that these latter are regional nominations, the appointments should be made conjointly by the county councils of each region, with it being a matter for each of them to decide the character of peers that should form their own delegation.

This would constitute a second chamber appointed by those who have been directly elected, in the first case chosen by our elected members of parliament to sit on the all-party committee for selecting peers on a national basis, in the second case chosen by the elected county councillors to represent their particular region. Peers of both variety will have been indirectly elected to the second chamber, with equal authority and similar duration of office – a unity of purpose and responsibility that should create no psychological division between the two groups, and without any of them having been directly elected.

The two elements that would still be missing from such a second chamber would be the European and the spiritual dimensions. The appointment of lords spiritual could well continue on the existing basis, but in participation perhaps with the all-party committee's quota for appointees. And I would hope that representatives of all the faiths which are to be found within this nation would find themselves nominated on a basis proportional to the prevalence of each faith.

With regard to the European dimension, this should emerge as the special responsibility of the regional peers, to establish cultural bonds with regions elsewhere throughout Europe, discovering where in Europe they might be doing things better than us and assisting them to learn from us where that might be applicable. For it is largely by these methods that the Europe of Regions will finally emerge.

It will be in these particular functions of the second chamber that we may expect Europe to start coming closer together, in harmony but with cultural diversity. I suggest that this is the legacy which we should be striving to hand down to our children. So while your lordships' house will remain strictly subordinate to another place, we might well discover that the quality of life, both in terms of our region and our continent, are very much in these hands.